MW00452096

Who Dares Wins Publishing
www.whodareswinspublishing.com

eBook ISBN: 978-1-935712-47-
Print ISBN 978-1-935712-48-0

Other Non-Fiction by Kristen Lamb
We Are Not Alone: The Writer's Guide to Social Media

Dedication

To my loving husband, Shawn. I couldn't do this without you. I will always cherish your words of encouragement that kept me going even when I thought I could write no more.

"It writes the words or it gets the hose."

Thanks for sending gluten-free crackers down in the basket. It's a little cold down here. Think I can get a blanket now?

I love you!

ARE YOU THERE BLOG?
It's Me, Writer

by

Kristen Lamb

Karima,
We are not
alone! Great to meet you.
Kristen Lamb

Table of Contents

Acknowledgements

I want to thank my husband, first of all, for supporting my dream. You know this guy has a sense of humor; he puts up with me. I also want to thank my long-time friend Gigi Salem for thinking of such an AWESOME title for this book. I am so grateful for my closest peeps who helped me shape this book and make it amazing. These folks are already tremendously busy, but they took time to read my book, help edit, offer feedback, and even write blurbs and contributions. I cannot thank them enough: James Scott Bell, James Rollins, Piper Bayard, Susan Bischoff, Kait Nolan, Peter St. Clair, Peter Koevari, Beth Barany, Laurie McClean, Tawna Fenske, Jody Hedlund, Chuck Wendig, Dr. Michael Bumagin, David Walker, and Jen Talty. You guys are amazing and I am possible THE most blessed person on the planet to know you guys.

I also want to thank all the loyal followers of my blog, my peeps on Facebook, and my tweeps on Twitter. None of this is possible without your support. You have all been such a wonderful team, and I suddenly feel the urge to start singing *Wind Beneath My Wings*...but I won't because I love you and hearing me sing could damage our friendship irreparably.

Praise for Kristen Lamb

New York Times bestselling author of The Doomsday Key, James Rollins

It's a new world out there for authors--a new paradigm of marketing, communication, and interaction--called social media. It's the new digital Wild West. And while we're all trying to reinvent the wheel, Kristen Lamb's informative and illuminating book, *ARE YOU THERE, BLOG? IT'S ME, WRITER* is a brilliant roadmap through this new frontier. It literally changed my view of social media, my role in it, and my responsibility to my readers. If you're an aspiring or established author, this is a must-read for all.

Nationally Best-Selling Author James Scott Bell

Are You There, Blog? It's Me, Writer is packed with practical, humorous advice on how to do -- and just as important, how NOT to do -- social media. Writers of every stripe will benefit from this timely and fun to read resource.

Laurie McLean, Literary Agent & Dean of San Francisco Writers University

Kristen Lamb is social media's Dorothy Parker for the 21st century. Laugh and learn. It's not an online traffic school; it's what you'll do in equal measures when you read *Are you there, Blog? It's Me, Writer*, by Kristen Lamb. A compilation of the best of her blog advice for writers, *Are You There* offers Kristen's hallmark common sense wisdom and down to earth lessons for writers who want to understand and participate in today's essential social networking. Ranging from missives on motivation to the nuts and bolts of how to use hashtags, Kristen lays it on the line in a no-nonsense style that is sure to entertain as well as enlighten. Bravo, Ms. Lamb! I'm there. I really am.

Author Chuck Wendig

Rest your head and let the Gospel According to Lamb guide you crazy writers through the tangled (and often insane) labyrinth that is social media. Lamb will tell you how to build your writer's platform not by cobbling together globules of fatty spam but rather by standing tall on your own two feet as a – *gasp*--*actual human being*. Is this essential reading? Say amen and hallelujah.

Romance Author Tawna Fenske

Kristen Lamb takes the fear factor out of social media for authors, making it fun, funny, and easy to understand. A must-read for writers at all stages of their careers!

Best-Selling Christian Romance Author Jody Hedlund

Kristen Lamb's social media advice for writers hits the bulls-eye every time. With a winning combination of wit and wisdom, Kristen shares relevant and applicable information that will help writers everywhere develop stronger social media skills and a broader web presence.

Paranormal Romance Author Kait Nolan

Lamb delivers the unvarnished truth that a writer's job is no longer merely to write...then takes the sting out by revealing with down-to-earth, unrivaled hilarity, how to do this social media thing right.

Warning: You just might bust a gut laughing.

Fantasy Author Peter Koevari

Whoever says that technical education can't be fun has to check out Kristen Lamb's book *Are You There, Blog? It's Me, Writer.* As a reader who loved her first book, *We Are Not Alone*, I looked forward to her next book and was impressed by its ability to make learning not *feel* like learning. Like all of Kristen's books, these lessons are easily understood by anyone. Kristen's books have revived my failing social media efforts and helped me create a platform that I not only enjoy, but that is showing positive growth. Her methods have helped me build relationships and enjoy opportunities that I would have otherwise never found.

Beth Barany, Author, Speaker, Book Coach, www.bethbarany.com

Kristen's new book, *Are You There, Blog, It's Me Writer*, gets me laughing right away. And I'm learning right away. For me that's priceless: fun, LOL funny and I'm learning something! By page 4, I'm on fire! Kristen's energy is contagious. I'm ready to tweak my blog right away. I keep stopping nearly every page to hop on Twitter or Facebook or do a search to help me connect with and understand my audience better. Her approach to blogging and creating our author platform is wonderfully clear-eyed, dosed liberally with her wacky humor, about what it really takes to succeed as an author today. And above all, Kristen is so on our side. (Thank you!) I learn something every single time I read one of Kristen's books, blog posts, or tweets. And I'm sure you will, too.

FOREWORD

In my job as a literary agent, I crisscross the country each year giving presentations at writers' conferences, chapters of national writing organizations, and other venues. I usually start off by stating emphatically, "Now is the best time EVER to be a writer," and I believe this statement is true with all my heart. But it is also the most challenging, frustrating and befuddling time to be a writer as well. And that's why Kristen Lamb is so important at this critical juncture in the publishing industry.

You see, publishing is going through the most disruptive upheaval in its history and writers need mentors to guide them through the long dark night into the breaking dawn of the new publishing paradigm. You think I jest. I do not.

It's difficult enough to find the time and stamina to write at all, let alone keep improving your craft, learn about Facebook, market and hand sell your books to an ever shrinking list of brick and mortar bookstores, network with readers and other writers, and indelibly stamp your author brand on the minds of readers and publishing professionals everywhere. Pshew! Just writing that sentence made me sweat! Think about having to actually do all those things.

Kristen's first book's title should further clarify her intent: *We Are Not Alone*. Kristen is one of those rare individuals who truly desires to help fellow writers learn from her mistakes and successes as she plunges into new digital publishing initiatives and lives to tell the tale. She offers up sage advice, gleaned from years in sales and writing, to writers hungry for guidance through this confusing maze of social media with all its potential and some very real pitfalls. This newest offering from Kristen, *ARE YOU THERE, BLOG? IT'S ME, WRITER*, is a compilation of her best social media advice for writers detailing how to turn these tools and techniques to your advantage. She never talks down to her visitors. She tells the bare truth.

But even that is not the core beauty of Kristen Lamb. Bluntly put: she is so funny you'll find yourself laughing as you learn, surprised when you come to the end of her book that the experience was not only painless, but indeed quite enjoyable. And I know you'll learn at least five things you didn't know before you read *Are You There*. She balances general tips on motivation with education about Twitter hashtags. She never gets too technical and her humor infuses every paragraph.

So, read this book. And after that, subscribe to her blog (I'm sure she'll give you that URL several times in the book because she practices what she preaches). Then buy *We Are Not Alone*. These three things alone will supercharge your writing career. They might even help you get an agent and succeed in traditional publishing as well.

Best of luck,

Laurie McLean, Agent at Larsen Pomada Literary Agents
(www.agentsavant.com)& Dean of San Francisco Writers University
(www.SFWritersU.com)

Introduction

Last summer, Who Dares Wins Publishing launched my debut book, *We Are Not Alone—The Writer's Guide to Social Media*. Thanks to loyal fans all over the world, it has been a tremendous success. Social media changes so quickly, it sometimes feels impossible to keep up, let alone get ahead. That's why, in addition to my book, I launched a blog I call WANA Wednesday…because I got tired of typing out We Are Not Alone Wednesday.

Yeah, I am all about efficiency (and a tad lazy).

The purpose of my blog was to give additional tips, tools and tactics to rock social media. I believe we learn best when we are having fun, and I hope you enjoy this selection of my favorite posts from the past year, plus some additional content you can only get here.

Are You There, Blog? It's Me, Writer is a collection of the best material to shove you out of your comfort zone, and help you laugh and learn at the same time. We must have a sense of humor about our mistakes and our challenges, or we will just want to give up.

Most of what I teach here will work on any social media platform. Rest assured that if Facebook is deleted or Twitter blows up, the lessons in this book will help you and your platform remain strong and continue to thrive no matter what social platform is hot. Technology changes, but human needs and emotions are timeless.

Social media should be enjoyable, and so should learning about it. I designed the flow of this book so that information would progress in a logical order. There are many themes and lessons you will see repeated but always in a new light and with a different twist. Not every selection is about social media (though most are). We are more than robots sitting in a chair cranking out word count. We are humans with hopes, dreams, fears, failures and baggage. Social media must be approached holistically in order to be successful, because our platform is a reflection of who we are.

Becoming a writer can be a terrifying experience, so I made sure to include content that I felt would "round out" your social media curriculum and prepare you for a brilliant future.

What better way to start this book, than with a Writer Reality Check?

Section One—Social Media and the 21st Century Writer

Writer Reality Check

If you are a fan of my book and blogs, then you know I am all about helping writers. You can count on me for the unvarnished truth. I know there are many people who believe they want to be writers. Hey, rock on! The more the weirder...I meant merrier. Yes...merrier.

Where was I? Oh yeah.

I feel our profession tends to be glamorized, and hopeful writers aren't aware of what to expect... really expect. So, when something comes flying at them from left field, they are unprepared and are watching fire ants roam over their tennis shoes instead of catching that giant hurdling ball headed straight for their head. Ooh! Just had a flashback. Did I mention that I sucked at sports?

Thus, before you resolve to become a writer, finish a novel, and take your craft more seriously there are some things to consider. I am going to give you a run-down of what to expect so you aren't caught unawares.

Expect:

That most people will not take you seriously. If you are waiting for your friends and family to line up and pat you on the back and throw you a parade, you will be sorely disappointed. In fact, when they see how euphorically happy you are, just expect for them to assume your writing group is really a cult and stage an intervention. Likely they will call in experts who perform deprogramming for loved ones lost to devil worshippers, Scientology, or that new retread of the Branch Davidians in south Texas. My advice? Look out for any white panel vans, and never leave your drinks unattended. You could wake up in a dark room wrapped in blankets going through a "rebirthing" procedure where you come into this world wanting to be something practical, like an engineer.

When people ask what you do, you need to tell them, "I am an author" or "I am a writer." Even if you don't have your book finished. This is going to sting. As long as you introduce yourself via your day job (other than writer), then you are telling your subconscious that you want to be that day job FOREVER. Don't even try to cheat with "I am an aspiring writer." Again, that is a subconscious cue, and twenty years later, you will still be "aspiring." Just go practice in the mirror and say a hundred times. "I am an author. I am an author."

If you want others to shut up and stop mocking you, just tell them they had better knock it off because there is a part for a nose-picking circus midget with mommy issues in your novel. Then they might agree to play nice.

You are a professional writer. To paraphrase Yoda, "There is no try, only do." Most people feel guilty saying they are a writer because they never write. In that case, you should feel guilty. Go nail your can to a chair and bust out at least a few words, you slacker. You are a writer, not an aspiring writer, but a *writer!* You can *aspire* to be a NY Times best-selling author, or to be known as *the* author who writes XYZ, but that doesn't make you an aspiring writer, that makes you a writer with firmly aligned goals. Then you have my permission to use the adjective aspiring. For all other times?

Screw aspiring. Aspiring is for pansies. Takes guts to be a writer.

Yes, other people will titter and roll their eyes, but you won't care. In the meantime, toughen up. You will need the skin of a rhino in this business. Do not look for outside approval. That is about as productive as looking for unicorns or Sasquatch.

To steal from the brilliant author Chuck Wendig, "Writing is not a parade of peppermint puppies." It is work. So here are some other things to expect that go with the job. Even professional authors cannot write eight hours a day. There are other important tasks that often will feel more like goofing off. Just get over it. I can spot writers who do not perform these routine duties, because their writing never improves. I used to think doing these tasks was "wasting time." My prose suffered. You know what real wasting time is? Writing crap. So to make our work better and better…

We need to read. This is essential. The best writers are avid readers. I read a fiction and a non-fiction book a week. One best-selling novel (genre doesn't matter) and one craft book. I walk around with my Nook in my purse. Standing in line at Target? Pick the long line and read five pages. Waiting at the doctor? The bank? Getting a pedicure? Make use of that time. Read. I read for 40 minutes on the elliptical at the gym. The Nook's ability to have giant font keeps me from throwing up and falling off. I also highly recommend using one of the single greatest inventions of modern man...the Post-It highlighter (not on your Nook/Kindle, but on the paper books).

We need to watch a lot of movies. The editor's mantra is, "Show. Don't tell." How do you learn to do that? Study. Watch actors. How do they portray the vast spectrum of human emotion? How do they portray characters? Study dialogue. Absorb speech patterns. Study structure. This is a faster method than reading. Study how the screenwriter raised the stakes. Why did the movie work? Why didn't it? This isn't as much a substitute for reading as it is an addition to reading. But we can watch movies with friends and family and yet still be "working."

How did the director portray normal world? Darkest moment? Study endings. You get the idea. Few jobs can claim that spending the day watching movies is actually work. Enjoy.

We must blog. Blogging creates good habits, and it is in the job description of the 21st century author. We can gripe and moan all we want, but that doesn't change reality. Reality is that writers with a platform are going to be more successful than writers who expect others to do everything for them. If you want to become a professional writer then you should love writing anyway, so this shouldn't be as big of a deal as most writers make it. Suck it up and put on Big Girl/Big Boy Pants. This is usually the biggest stumbling block, but now I am here so no more excuses. I am going to make blogging FUN!

We need to spend time on social media. This is like the watching movies and reading thing. Yes, being on social media is work. Now if we are just goofing off and sending people farm animals, then yes, we are goofing off. But if we are blogging and spending time on Twitter and FB networking with other writers, published authors and people in the publishing industry, that is called marketing.

Additionally, I have found some of the best articles and blogs on the craft via Twitter and other bloggers. Social media gives us countless tools to improve our skills daily.

We need to write. Eventually all of this boils down to what it is we do...we write. As I said earlier, we can't always be writing and the writing part, while the most important, doesn't take up the most time. Reading, planning, researching, outlining, editing, revising, marketing are all parts of the job, too. Yet, ultimately, we need to sit our keisters down and WRITE. Not rocket-science here.

We need to learn to employ tough love. I can tell you from experience that you will have to be tough with friends and family. They aren't used to you having a second job. They will miss you being around all the time and they will need to be retrained. And I am telling you now that they will not "get" you so don't expect them to. Just be kind and consistent, and if they still don't get the hint, invest in a caffeinated meth-addicted ferret to guard the door for you while you write.

It may be a good idea to introduce your plans to your family in the following way:

"Hey, I sold all our worldly belongings, and the VW van will be here in the morning to take us to live at the Prophet's commune in New Mexico. Your names are now Rainbow and Starchild. Ha ha ha ha, just kidding. Mommy is now a writer."

Regardless how you break the news, it needs to be done. Being a writer is tough work, but it is a whole lot of fun.

***

Now that you've had a little reality check, I want us to shift gears. I am going to do my best to help you understand goal-setting better. We are wise to approach social media with a plan, but it needs to be a plan that doesn't end with us on the roof with a chocolate cake and a shotgun. It needs to be fun and fit into our existing lives. Our spouses, kids, dust bunnies aren't going to go away just because we need to market.

The lion's share of this book is, of course, social medium of blogging. However, social media is a reflection of who we are. If we are unfocused and chaotic, that will spill into how we handle ourselves on social media. It's a noble goal to reach for your dreams, but I want to give you the tools to enjoy the journey, too. Thus, without further ado...

Planning for Success

Remember the feeling? It's New Year's Eve, and you are standing on the threshold of a shiny new year. It's almost as good as getting new school supplies. The smell of virgin paper not yet touched by a ballpoint. A new start. No mistakes. Nothing but potential.

Okay, so if you are anything like me, your initial New Year's Resolutions might look something like this.

1. Lose 20 pounds by February 1st
2. Run a marathon
3. Go to gym 5 hours a day
4. Win the ~~Nobel~~ Pulitzer by my birthday
5. Save 85% of my income
6. Go on vacation to Bora Bora (Note to Self: Look up actual location of Bora Bora)
7. Clean out garage
8. Paint house inside and out
9. Finally have all my socks match
10. Write 3 award-winning novels by summer

There is something about facing a new year that instills us with such hope that we lose all touch with reality (and we hadn't even started drinking yet). It's great to set goals, but most of the time we are our own worst enemy.

Odds are, if you are a fan of my blogs, you are likely a writer, you want to learn to write better or this is a condition of your parole. Regardless, all of us need to learn to set effective goals and learn habits that will keep us from sabotaging our own success.

Last year was one of my best years of all time. I reached many goals. Why? Because I learned some good lessons and applied them consistently. I hope to do even better this year. So, I am going to pass these lessons on to you and hope that you will benefit as well.

1. Grant Permission to be Imperfect—Perfectionism is a noble trait which, taken to the extreme, can serve as an excuse for mediocrity and a mask for fear. Perfectionists tend to be self-saboteurs (I would know nothing about this; *whistles innocently*). We perfectionists nit-pick over every single detail, often at the expense of the big picture. Perfection is noble, so it makes a great shield. I mean, we just don't believe in churning out shoddy work, right? Um…maybe. Or maybe we have a fear of failure, or even a fear of success. So long as nothing is ever complete, we never have to face our demons and can happily fritter away our days perfecting our scenes and dialogue.

Here's the deal. No publishing house ever published half of a perfect book.

2. Give Baby Steps a Chance—All or nothing thinking, a close relative of perfectionism, can tank the best projects. It is so easy to fall into this trap of, "If I can't do X, then I do nothing at all." Baby Steps are still steps. It's like the question, "How do you eat a whale? One bite at a time." Small steps, over time, with consistency add up. It's sort of like working out. We can choose to show up January 2nd at 5 a.m. and work out three hours, but that is a formula to end up sore, injured and burned out.

Often when I go to the gym I am so tired I want to die. I used to be the person who tried to do too much too soon, only to end up sick or injured. Two years ago, I made a key change in my attitude. Now when I go to the gym I tell myself, "All I have to do is ten minutes walking on the treadmill. Ten minutes. If I still feel tired, horrible, sick, fatigued, disenchanted, etc. I can stop, go home, and climb back into bed." In two years, I have only stopped twice. Usually all I need is to push past that initial wall and then I am off like a rocket.

Same with writing. Make small goals.

I will write 15 minutes.

I will write 100 words.

Sometimes all we need is a little momentum. Can't rev the motor if we never turn the key. A good way to get going is to use kitchen timers. Set the clock and write for 30 minutes. I use sticky notes and set my big goal then I divide it in half. One sticky note is on the left-hand side of my monitor (starting count). I then place the half-way point in the middle, and I am not allowed a break until I make that number (even if all I write is pigeon poo). The finish line is on the right.

Getting started is always the hardest part. I generally find that if I can make it to the mid-point, I am golden.

3. Establish Accountability—Critique groups and partners are a great way to achieve some accountability. It is easy to blow off writing when it is just us, but when we will be a letdown to others? Different story. This is one of the reasons I LOVE blogging. Blogging has done so much to change my character. I adore my followers. I love helping. I also love hearing feedback. I feel my fans have given me their trust and that I need to always put my best effort forward. The funny thing is that this change in my writing habits has bled into other areas of my writing. Sort of like, when you get in the habit of going to the gym, you also start noticing that you take the stairs or don't mind parking at the back of the parking lot.

This is why writing down our goals is imperative. If nothing else, it is a cue to our subconscious that we are committed to something. We will feel a lot more conviction if we write out a goal than if we decide to let it float around our gray matter.

I would even advise taking it to the next step and sharing your goals with others. I feel this is why so many writers have a hard time saying aloud, "I am a writer." To say it means we have to own it and that people will be watching. We are going to invite a whole other level of accountability and people will notice if we are goofing off. However, I say that accountability is the best way to reach your dreams faster, so bring it on!

4. Small Change Will Grow into Big Change—Good habits have a way of filtering through our lives. I have a saying, "Smaller truths reveal larger truths." We don't have to do mind-blowing alterations in our routines to start seeing real change in our lives. I guarantee that if you just start making your bed in the morning, other things will fall in line. Soon, you will notice that your bedroom is neater, and then the kitchen. As your house gets tidier, so does your purse and your car, and so on and so forth. Just start with small writing goals and I guarantee that bigger, better changes will follow.

5. Understand that Feelings LIE—Modern pop psychology loves to ask about our feeeelings all the time. Feelings are important, but they are a lousy compass to guide our actions. Why? Feelings can be affected by so many things—fatigue, diet, too much sleep, too little sleep, jerks at the office, kid toys underfoot, PMS, hormones, too much caffeine, not enough caffeine, cat vomit in our house slippers, and on and on and on. If I can pass on any lesson that will change your life, it is for you to understand that your feelings will almost always take the path of least resistance. If we are going to accomplish anything in life, we cannot let our feelings have a vote.

I blog whether I feel like it or not. I don't wait until I feel like writing to sit my *tuchus* in a chair. Feelings can be the enemy and steal your dreams. The Crappy Excuse Trolls and Procrastination Pixies will capitalize on your feelings and do everything in their power to convince you that you will get to it later when you feel like it. Shut them down. Don't give your feelings a vote.

The best way to shut down your feelings is to make lists of goals. I make lists every day and it keeps me focused. I can be exhausted, disenchanted, disillusioned, but it doesn't matter. I look to the list. It's like my earlier example of the gym. I say, "Okay, I will just do the first three." Funny thing is that once I get started, I usually keep going. Like most things in life, overcoming that initial inertia is the hardest part. Lists keep us focused and don't give feelings a say.

6. Make a Plan—There is a saying in sales, *Fail to plan, plan to fail*. A good plan will keep you focused, accountable, and give you clear benchmarks to measure success. I recommend buying NY Times Best-Selling Author Bob Mayer's *Warrior Writer From Writer to Published Author*. He teaches how to craft a plan for a writing career. In fact Who Dares Wins Publishing, is all about helping authors succeed. To back this up, WDWPUB is almost always running a special, and you can order a special bundle package of *Warrior Writer From Writer to Published Author* along with my agent-recommended book *We Are Not Alone—The Writer's Guide to Social Media* AND Bob's *Novel Writer's Toolkit* that will take you from idea to finished product. These three books are the basic pillars to a successful career. I also recommend the Write It Forward Workshops. For $20 a workshop, you can learn everything about self-publishing, writing a novel, social media, and on and on…all from the comfort of your home and for less than the cost of eating out one meal.

In the end? *Just Do It*. Put that slogan on Post-It notes and paper your house if you must. Put a Troll doll on your computer to remind you to be wary of Crappy Excuse Trolls in your midst. If any of you are new and don't know the M.O. of the Crappy Excuse Trolls and

Procrastination Pixies then read on, because they make 12% commission off your shattered dreams. We will talk about them in a while. For now?

Remember:

1. Grant Permission to Be Imperfect
2. Give Baby Steps a Chance
3. Establish Accountability
4. Trust that Small Change will Grow into Big Change
5. Understand that Feelings LIE
6. Make a Plan

Doing these basic steps can make all the difference between failure and success, magnificence and mediocrity. I want you to be a successful author and still have a family that speaks to you. Good luck!

Now that we have discussed a little about goal-setting, we need to look at approach. Content is meaningless if we blow the execution.

The Most Effective Social Marketing Tool—Kindness

Spam! Spam! Spam! Spam!

I love SPAM. In fact, there are few things that can make me feel more special than spam. Okay, form letters, pop-ups and auto-tweets, but that's all. I love it when someone takes the time to program his or her computer to send me a "personalized" message—Dear Valued Follower, go to my link. That makes my day almost as much as telemarketers. Hey, I said "almost."

Let's not get crazy.

No, I haven't gone crazy, but it seems that many writers do the second they realize they must market themselves in order to survive the shifting paradigm in publishing. We go from nice, sweet, fun writers to morphing into that weird third cousin we stopped talking to after she joined Amway.

One of the reasons I decided to write social media books for writers is that I see these mistakes all the time. Worse, I see well-meaning writers who are just trying to be professional, PAYING people for software and books and techniques that make them about as appealing as a pop-up ad.

Now, do not misunderstand me. I am not saying these other social media folk are wrong. Frequently, they aren't. However, many of them are trying to lay a standard business-marketing template over a writer's career, and it just doesn't fit. Why? For a number of reasons, but the largest is that, despite what TV commercials tell us, we really do NOT expect a personal relationship with our insurance company. Seriously. I do not call up USAA when my mother has me ready to pull out my hair or when I feel insecure about my thighs or when the dog throws up on my new book and eats my glasses.

Okay, I did, but they threatened to raise my rates to include therapy.

Many benevolent social media folk know how to rock it hard when it comes to the regular business world. In the regular business world mailers, form letters, unsolicited coupons and promotions work. I know. I used to be in sales. When writers use them? They usually are just annoying tactics that will actually have the opposite results more often than not.

For instance…

This past week on Facebook, I approved a friend request for another writer. Within MINUTES, I had four other e-mails. "Here is my website! Go to my blog! Look at my book! Here is a discount! Pass on to all of your friends and let me show them how to blah blah blah!" It made me regret I'd ever befriended this person. Rather than it being like Starbucks, "Here is a coupon for a free Frappuccino" (awesome); it sounded more like, "Me, me, me, me, me! Look at meeeeee! I have vested nothing in this relationship other than clicking *Add Friend* and then cutting and pasting, but now I want something from you. Time! Attention! Promotion! Money!"

I always talk about the heart of the servant. Be genuinely interested in other people and the promotion will come. Genuine promotion that really will speak to others. Most people will feel the need to reciprocate if we are always positive and authentic. Our motive should always be pure—do something authentically kind—because people can smell manipulation from a mile away, and who likes being manipulated? Nobody.

I know it seems counterintuitive when you have marketing folk shouting about "top of mind" and "numbers" and "exposure." Those things matter, but writers would be wise to approach marketing differently from Crocs Sandals or Domino's Pizza. On social media, relationships are key to building a platform and a readership. They see our name and see our face, but we need to work to earn the reader's trust.

Ack! Work!

Yes, but no more work than the time it takes to go SPAM a hundred people. In addition, this method will bear a better harvest and create a platform that will stand the test of time because it is founded on relationship. If you want something from others, then freely give from the start.

But Kristen! I AM giving. I just sent them the past ten issues of my "Romance Times" newsletter for free where I give them excerpts of my unpublished novel and a bookmark they can print off on their home computer.

Nooooo. That is taking. Giving is when you take your time to read their blog, to repost their story and to congratulate their writing goal on Twitter. Giving is when you write a nice review of someone else's book unsolicited and expecting nothing in return.

Sow kindness and generosity of your own spirit and you will be pleasantly surprised at the results. Authentic kindness is so inspiring to others that it frequently moves them to do the same thing.

As an example—I was up early one morning on Twitter. On my TweetDeck I saw this woman Donna who lived in London, England post her first chapters of her book on her blog on #writegoal. I wasn't even following Donna, and didn't know her from a hole in the ground. But, I was once a new writer so I took time to read her chapter and comment, even though it put me almost an hour behind my schedule. Donna immediately followed me, and I offered her my e-mail so I could help her. One-on-one. No money. No asking her to buy my book. I didn't even tell her about my book. I just remembered how hard it was being new and how much difference my mentor made in me. I paid it forward.

All I wanted from her was that she be teachable and that she work hard, and Donna has done both (no money and no stipulations of buying stuff). I added her to a new style of critique group I'd started to help her construct her novel, since one of the problems I noticed was that although she showed talent, she didn't understand how to plot and was drifting all over the place.

Running Donna through the on-line workshop put me even MORE behind, in that now I had to read and edit the assignments I gave her. With a book due and a day job I could barely squeeze the time, but I saw something promising in Donna, so I made it work…even though I had to do so at the expense of my free time.

But you know what happened?

I now have a writer who is light-years ahead of where she would have been had I not taken the time to intervene. She reposts every blog I post, comments on my blogs, and was giddy to make all of her friends follow me. Donna not only attended the DFW Writers Conference (where I was teaching), but she even recruited one of her girlfriends from AUSTRALIA to come with her. They both flew in from thousands of miles away, and we had an amazing time.

Two $400 conference seats sold, and I wasn't even selling.

I now am friends with Donna and all of her network, and it means something. I truly believe that Donna is the largest reason I have gained such a massive fan base in the UK; a harvest from that original seed of kindness.

I think most of us writer-folk aren't fond of "selling," but we do like reading and giving our opinions, feedback and support. That is the best kind of marketing. Focus on acts of kindness—one per day. They don't have to be big or massively time-consuming kindnesses. Spend the same time you would spend trolling for people to send form letters and find a way to encourage or help them instead.

Let's leave all the gadgets and promos to Chili's and iPod. We have real friends to make. You will be glad you did.

Maybe now it is easier to breathe and feel confident to make pals on social media and know you are still working. Gasp! We have already answered some tough questions, so time to tackle another biggie.

Are You Sending the Right Message? 3 Bad Habits that Can KILL Your Social Media Marketing

Let's take some time to address some behaviors I am seeing on social media that can actually do more harm than good. These tactics work for traditional marketing, but will make you a pariah at light speed on social media. We are going to address the Top Three Bad Habits:

1. Form letters and auto-replies
2. Reposting your own content over and over
3. Failing to reciprocate and engage with others

I am not writing this to embarrass anyone. If you have been guilty of any of these, there is good reason. These are tactics employed in traditional marketing. They do not translate well into the realm of social media. Thus, before venturing any further, let's look at the old ways of marketing versus the new so you will be able to see more clearly why our approach must be different for social media.

I think one huge mistake all of us make is we risk falling back into that old way of thinking about marketing. We believe we must do it all on our own, so we feel propelled to go make hundreds and thousands of friends and blitz out our information over and over to be "good, responsible little marketers." That is a major fallacy when it comes to social media.

In traditional marketing, a brand was passively received, thus the brand had to be controlled and one-dimensional to keep from confusing the masses receiving the image plastered on billboards, placards, magazines and broadcast on radios and TV. A brand had to be static and fixed because any deviation could confuse the consumer and dilute the message.

Just Do It.

Nowadays, branding is highly organic and always in flux, namely because we are in the Information Age. We are constantly being fed real-time images and impressions via YouTube, Twitter, FB, and blogs. Not only are we being fed these impressions, but then we often take them in, filter them, then recycle/repackage them when we resend them out to our community in the form of our opinions. This is why our marketing approach must be fluid and dynamic. We want people to take in our message, like it and deliver it to their communities in a positive way.

To accomplish this, our approach must be modified.

Marketing is now in the hands of the audience. Thus, now it becomes critical what the audience thinks of us, because that will affect how they handle our message.

For instance, 20 years ago, it was far less important whether an author was a nice person or not. Who cared? Could she write? An author could have been the biggest jerk on the planet and it didn't matter so long as she didn't do anything that made national headlines. She could hand in her books, and then the marketing/PR people controlled what impression went out to the masses, if any. Writers could live quiet lives of obscurity, and it really didn't affect their book sales.

Now?

What a writer's fans think of her as a person influences her marketing. Now, this author can choose to do nothing, and the PR people will keep sending out her crafted image. But what if she wants more? She needs to get in the mix. The more an author interacts with her fan base in a positive way, the more likely those fans will pass on her messages in a positive light. By continual personal and positive interaction, an author can influence groups of people to extend her marketing influence. How? She has recruited her fans and followers to be part of her team. Book sales and promotion have now become a collective endeavor.

Traditional marketing was a demographic-numbers game. We threw enough stuff (content, mailers, coupons) at a particular wall (demographic) and then hoped something stuck that generated word-of-mouth or "buzz" that would translate into readers and then into fans. This tactic works in traditional marketing, but often breaks down on social media. The companies who do the best on social media have a different approach for social media that appreciates the consumer's participation and need for community.

Same with writers.

We do better focusing on authentic, positive relationships and then enlisting others to carry our message. We don't have to have 6000 friends to reach 6000 people. We must have a good amount of authentic interactions with others who will then carry our message to their networks. Do this correctly, and eventually their network will become our network and our influence will spread exponentially. In social media, it works better to employ relationships to spread our message, not fancy software that can target customers and SPAM them, but, trust me, this method is way more fun anyway.

This is why the three offenders I noted at the beginning are so offensive. Remember, what others on social media think of you as a person will affect the end results of your marketing. So:

1.   **Beware the Form Letter/Auto-Reply**

Traditional marketing sought to add a quick personal touch to a static agenda. That's why when you get form letters in the mail; a company will often insert your name. We know the people at Best Buy didn't sit and type individual little us a letter, but the personal touch does create a tad bit of rapport. However, this is a static message from a faceless company. When Best Buy sends me coupons and sales, they are not counting on my liking them, taking the mailer and copying it and then mailing it to my network of friends and family. On social media? You are definitely depending on the recipients of your message to become bearers of your message. Form letters do not work. Auto replies are impersonal and most people find them annoying. Writers are not Starbucks. Even major corporations who use social media well will employ a personal approach. On Twitter, Comp USA and Starbucks resemble a chat with customer service. Even the big guys know that spamming people is risky and annoying.

2.   **Repost Redundancy**

We all get excited about our blogs that we work hard to write, but reposting over and over and over can be very counterproductive. There used to be a self-published writer on Twitter who constantly posted his blogs with every writer hashtag imaginable…over and over and over.

Note: Hashtags (#) placed with key words are filtered into specific groups on Twitter. It is like a club on Twitter, bound by a #. So everyone who has #amwriting after a tweet, their message will

go in a special column.

Back to my point.

This writer's blogs were actually pretty good, but after the fifteenth time in one day of him tooting his own horn, I wanted to scream. His constant self-promotion hogged up most of the #writegoal column, which I actually like to follow. So instead of me seeing other writers and their goals so I could congratulate them or interact...all I would see was this guy...over....and over...and...seriously?...yeah, over again. This was the wrong way to be top of mind. And what was this making me (and others) think of him as a person? I still believe he genuinely wanted to help and share, but that was certainly NOT what he was portraying. Eventually enough people complained, and this author was booted from Twitter, and banned from using hashtags.

3.   Attention Hogs Don't Get the Right Attention

Platforms are tough to build, and on social media we need to help each other. This point actually is a natural segue from my previous point. We always need to be mindful to post and repost the work of others. If we don't, others will rapidly resent us and that doesn't help anyone. Other people have valuable information to contribute. Let them. In traditional marketing, it is all about you. In social media marketing? It is about your network. The more you share, the greater the reward.

In WANA, I give a formula for effective interaction on social media. *1/3 Information*—blogs, articles, etc. *1/3 Reciprocation*—edify others. Repost their links, blogs, and book signings. You want your stuff reposted? Have to give to receive. And finally *1/3 Conversation*. People are on social media for community, so interact. Congratulate people who make their deadlines. Comment on their posts. Engage. Form letters and SPAM are not effective like they can be in traditional marketing and can actually just alienate the very people we desire to reach.

Social media should be fun. There are many wonderful people out there, so go make some friends. Ah...but hold on there, Sparky. Don't get too excited.

The Secret to Social Media Success—Slow & Steady Wins the Race

I once participated in an open forum discussing book marketing using social media. There was a weird technology glitch that hindered my participating, and it seemed that out of the woodwork all of these other experts swarmed in to take my place. I know they were excited and meant well, but it brought up an interesting point.

We need to always consider who is doing the selling.

Social media people love what? Social media! They know every gidget and gadget and whats-it and gizmo and they are awesome at what they do. But what do they do? They do social media. I think this can become a huge problem for a writer trying to learn social media in order to build a platform.

Think of it this way. Most social media experts are like people who do personal training for a living. They live to work out because it is what they do and how they make a living. They are tan, with six-pack abs and 6% body fat. Can we be that way too? Sure. A personal trainer would be happy to show you her lifestyle. All we have to do is get up at 4:00 every morning and hit the gym. Then after work go for a run and do some yoga. Oh and we need to pre-make all of our meals so we aren't tempted to eat anything other than egg whites, tuna fish and broccoli. Oh and here is a list of supplements and powders and drinks and gels and….

AARRGGGHHH!!!!!

Okay, maybe we would just like to be able to wear something other than stretchy pants.

Personal trainers are a happy energetic lot, and they will tell you all the benefits of eating algae and tofu and being detoxed with the latest cleanse. They want us to be just as happy and healthy as they are. Yet, there is often a huge problem. We might desire to be 6% body fat and a size -0, but we have jobs and families and need to sleep.

A person who makes her living as a personal trainer can live this way because it is already in sync with her goals and her life. For the mother of two who works as a teacher, becoming fitness model thin is a HUGE time commitment with a lot of sacrifice. Can she do it? Of course. But for most women, just being a healthy weight is already a struggle. If we shoot for fitness model fitness, we likely will give up before we ever see real benefit.

Social media experts do social media for a living. So to advise a writer that they need to be on Facebook, Twitter, Tumblr, LinkedIn, Flickr, YouTube, del.ici.ous., Squidoo, Digg, and on and on and on is natural for them. Why? Because that is their life and what they DO. They do social media because they love it and like the fitness trainer, they want us to love it that much, too.

Back the social media forum. The host of the Q & A then asked me what sites I recommended most for writers and before I could answer, an expert swooped in to do it for me. He eagerly suggested that a writer needed to blog and be on Facebook and Twitter and then eventually add LinkedIn...

WHAT?

I finally managed to eke in a, "Why would a paranormal romance author benefit from a site dedicated to business professionals?"

It stopped him dead in his tracks.

When I suggested an author stick to two main platforms (FB and Twitter) and a blog, it was like I had committed social media sacrilege. I recommended the author profile the readers she wanted to reach and then gain a solid footing on those platforms.

Don't get me wrong, he was very nice, but the thought hadn't occurred to him. Why?

Is it because social media people sit up all night thinking of ways to make life difficult for writers? Of course not! These folks are great, but they are coming from the perspective of social media expert, not the perspective of a writer who needs to have time and energy left over to write more books. This really nice social media guy didn't get why writers wouldn't love to be on a zillion sites, because for him social media is the means and the end.

I am a writer first. I love social media and I love teaching writers how to use it in a way that doesn't totally disrupt their lives. I think that there are a lot of cool sites out there and if you love social media then ROCK ON! Yet, when planning our social media approach, we have to be careful. Social media works best when we forge relationships, when we create networks of people who know us, support us, and are emotionally vested in us. How can we achieve that across 9 different platforms?

So 3 Tips:

1.   Be very careful not to mistake traditional marketing with social marketing.

Having a "presence" on 20 different sites so you and your book can get "exposure" is traditional marketing. Be careful about relying too much on that. People are gravitating to social media, in part, to escape the constant bombardment. You will, in my opinion, be better off interacting on one or two platforms consistently so others can get to know you and be vested in your future.

2.   Use logic to calculate ROI.

What's ROI? Return on Investment. What is your time worth? Focus on what will eventually translate into sales. Don't get on a site just to claim you are on it. If you write NF, then LinkedIn is useful, but if you write YA is it really worth time you could be spending on FB?

For example, I was asked about how I felt about Goodreads. Goodreads is a site where people share what they have read; get recommendations about what to read, etc. A cool site and, if, you have the time, sally forth. But let's get perspective. Great. A bazillion people put you in their "To Read List." Okay, cool. Doesn't mean a thing until they purchase a book. Handing out a bunch of free books can work against you, and that is a topic for another time. Just take it for what it is…potential. Focus where you are likely to get results….relationships.

3.   Make small consistent deposits.

Writers are an excitable bunch. When we find out about social media, we are notorious for running out and joining every site on the web. We blog every day and tweet until we wear out our tweeter…then we crash and DIE. Hey, I've been there. I am a writer too, remember? I once had a Flickr account, four Twitter accounts, two MySpace pages, 2 FB pages, three blogs, a LinkedIn account, a Goodreads account…and a prescription for Xanax.

Part of why I wrote *We Are Not Alone—The Writer's Guide to Social Media* was to help other writers learn from my mistakes.

Practice the principle òf parsimony. Less is often more.

Small, consistent deposits. Like working out. We don't have to work out four hours a day to be healthy. If we want to do a bit more than the average bear, we can hire a personal trainer. Ah, same with social media. We can't write great books and be on every single social media site….but we can hire these super enthusiastic social media experts to build it bigger for us ;). In the meantime, though, we have to do our own work.

A word of caution; platforms take years to build, but only seconds to destroy. Let's practice some common sense and good manners so that we can keep the focus on us and our writing.

Social Media Savvy—The Art of Making Others Feel Welcome

I teach, specifically, social media for writers. Duh. But seriously, writers are unique. Our social media presence is different than a business or even a casual user. We straddle both worlds, and often we feel as if we are in social limbo. We have to make sure to be friendly and personable and interact, but we also must remember that we are a business and have an image to build and a reputation to protect.

In my other book *We Are Not Alone*, content was my primary focus. For me, walking a reader through signing up for a Twitter profile wasn't nearly as important as coaching that individual on what to do once she began to "tweet." What should she say? Before our hot little fingers can dash across the keyboard, we need to engage our brain and T.H.I.N.K.

Ask:

Is it TRUE?

Is it HELPFUL?

Is it INFORMATIVE?

Is it NECESSARY?

Is it KIND?

I didn't invent this acronym, but it sure is useful. Social media is, above all else, social. Yet, it is easy to get lulled into a false sense of security when we are sitting in the privacy of our homes wearing Sponge Bob pajama pants and monkey slippers. Maybe that's just me. My point is that our main goal as writers is to use social media in order to build a platform of individuals who know us, like us and support us. To do this, we must be personable, kind and genuinely interested in others.

We must also be cognizant that everything we do is a calculated business decision. We are free to do anything we want on social media.

We can gripe about other authors, agents, and publishing houses. We can grouse and get into Twitter fights. We can tweet dirty jokes and rant about the economy, the war, and the state of public education. We are free to do all of these things. No writer police will show up at our door and haul us away. But, even though we are free to do all these things, we must ask ourselves if it is wise from a business perspective.

I advise writers to stay away from polarizing subjects. Sex, politics and religion are topics guaranteed to quickly divide people and create ill will. Therefore, unless these subjects are part of our platform, it is just a good idea to steer clear.

Gasp. Why, Kristen, we have beliefs and a faith and a viewpoint!

Okay, fair enough. So do I. But I imagine most of you are a lot like me. I like being friends with all kinds of people, not just those folk with the same beliefs. I want all kinds of people in my corner, buying my books and wishing for my success, not only those who believe the same things I do. As writers trying to build a platform, we are wise to think of social media like one giant social gathering, and that means we need to be great hosts. Others are a guest on our blog or in our space, so we should show them kindness by making them as comfortable as possible.

Few people are logical. We operate on emotions. I once had a writer ask me to evaluate his blog. It was a 1200 word ranting about a politically volatile topic. I felt sick to my stomach by the third sentence and I literally felt bludgeoned by the third paragraph. Do I believe the writer intended that response? Of course not. He was being bold and passionate and blogging about something he believed fiercely was right. Nevertheless, I would wager that, for at least 50% of his audience, reading that blog would likely rank up with dental surgery without anesthesia as not an experience we care to repeat.

If he is a fiction author, then what did that blog do for his platform? It split it clean down the middle by alienating half of his following. Any comments on the blog would also be split. One side would think he was a grand ideologue, and the other half would want his head…and would likely tell everyone they knew to steer clear of him and anything he wrote.

Remember our little acronym, T.H.I.N.K.? Was it true? For him, yes. Was it helpful? He certainly thought so. Was it informative? Oh, indeed! Ah, but was it necessary? For a political author? Heck yes! But for a fiction author? Probably not. Thus, this author could fracture his following needlessly by blogging on a divisive subject that did nothing to support his fiction platform. For a political writer, this is great blogging. For a novelist, this can quickly turn into a needless travesty.

Emerson once said that good manners are made up of petty sacrifices. Am I asking writers to give up who they are and what they believe in? Not at all. But I do firmly believe in your talent as writers. Surely those of you gifted enough to create entirely new worlds are talented enough to be yourself in a way that always makes others feel welcome and included. Yes, it takes more work and takes self-discipline. And, yes, sometimes it will be maddening to not bait to some other party's on-line rant. However, think of the goodwill we will be spreading to others. Our tweets, blogs, and status updates will be a welcome refuge, a safe-haven from a world blighted with pessimism.

Humans crave positive feelings. We can't get enough of them. Blogs that educate, encourage and inspire? Those are the blogs that gain our subscriptions our loyalty and our referrals. Ben Franklin once said, "If you argue and rankle and contradict you may achieve a victory sometimes; but it will be an empty victory because you never get your opponent's good will."

When it comes to how we will use social media, we all must make one key decision. Would we like to have an academic victory or a follower's good will? I would endorse good will any day of the week. Here's to making the world a brighter place one post, one blog and one tweet at a time.

Kristen Lamb

Maximize our Social Media Impact—Understanding Influence

One of the biggest complaints I hear about social media is that writers believe they have no time. I am going to share a little secret. We have plenty of time if we do it properly. The problem—I will say it again—is that too many writers are approaching social media like traditional marketing instead of social marketing. When we try to apply traditional marketing tactics, we will be spread too thinly to be effective and, truthfully, can do more harm than good. There is a key difference between traditional marketing (market norms) and social marketing (social norms).

Social marketing capitalizes on networking. Embrace the great news. We don't have to do everything alone! Traditional marketing will tempt you to be on every last social media site and make a bazillion "friends," yet all those "friends" will likely not be too vested in your success. So please trust me. A smaller network of effective influencers is far more powerful than a thousand followers who add little social media value.

What is social media value?

Well, these are the members of your social grid who participate actively and add good content to the Internet community. We are going to talk about the different kinds of influencers in a moment. Find these key individuals, and there are no limits to your digital reach. These influencers are platform-building GOLD and your most valuable asset.

How do you find the key influencers?

There are a number of ways to pinpoint your major influencers, but it is tricky. Why? Because unlike direct marketing or old-fashioned PR, the goal of social media is to influence entire groups of people. We aren't just targeting one individual, but rather the individual and his/her surrounding community. This is one of the reasons that, unlike direct marketing, the overall effectiveness of social media is not as easy to measure. There are some SIM (Social Influence Marketing) metrics that one can run, and companies that can help you locate your referent influencers, but I don't know that they are all that helpful for authors wanting to build a platform.

Yeah, you are going to have to do some work. Sorry. But I'll help you make it fun.

Writers are different from companies doing social media. That was my impetus for writing a book for authors. Not all tools that work well in the corporate world cross over.

Unlike General Motors or Coca Cola, most of us are a one-man operation. We don't have a marketing department, and we also have a different kind of product. The CEO of Toyota is not responsible for making every car that comes off the assembly line. Yet, until we become brand names and too big to handle all our own writing, we are responsible for the material that hits the bookstore shelves.

We cannot outsource our social media content (blogs, articles, excerpts, commentary, group activity, etc.) like, say, Miller Beer or Smoothie King.

The plain fact of the matter is that the more you participate in social media, the better the results. And when I say participate, that means strategized participation (mixed with fun) with clear end goals. I give a detailed step-by-step how-to in WANA, and I am working on a new social media book with updated information. Thinking of calling it, *Stop Sending Me Farm Animals Before I Send You a Digital Mob Boss to Shoot Your Internet Connection, Roll It in a Rug and Dump It in the River So You Can Make Your Word Count.*

I dunno. Maybe a little too long.

But basically, you do need a plan. In order to have a plan, you must understand the players if you hope to identify those who can maximize your influence, thereby minimizing the time you spend on social media. Not all users are treated equally. They are divided into categories that correspond with the influence they wield in their networks.

Expert Influencer—is just what it says. These are the authorities in a certain subject, and people look to these experts for information, advice, and guidance. The experts are heavyweights when it comes to influencing the decisions of those in their networks. Expert influencers usually have a picture of themselves as their icon. They also generally have huge following that number in the thousands or tens of thousands, depending on the platform. Also, a quick glance to their website (which is usually denoted in the bio) will give you a clear picture that this person is an expert in her field. Oprah. Enough said.

Referent Influencer—is in the person's social network and exercises influence. Referent influencers are a little trickier to figure out. They generally have a fairly large following, but not always. Quality and quantity are not the same thing.

So how do you figure out the referent influencers? You have to participate so you can pay attention. For the most part the referent influencers are highly active on social media and thus usually have a larger following than the casual user, but maybe not as large as the expert. Yet, it is their level of meaningful activity that makes them essential to have in your network. They post frequently and are well-known, liked, and respected for good content. People around them trust them for good stuff. These are the people you miss when they take a day off.

In my opinion, referent influencers are the most valuable. Why? First, it is easier to get close to them and befriend them and gain their support. If you write a blog about parenting (as part of your NF book platform), what are the odds of becoming part of Oprah's inner circle? Referent influencers are far more approachable.

Secondly, referent influencers are genuine and personal and thus exercise tremendous authority. I think that people tend to trust these influencers almost as much the experts, if not more. Why? Well, human nature. We like things from the proverbial mouth of the horse. We can't really be sure Oprah picks her Books of the Month for herself. She may have gatekeepers who at least narrow the field of choices. But, Suzy Lit-Girl, freelance writer and respected book reviewer who posts every week and has over 3000 people in her immediate network (including big authors and publishing houses) is easier to win to your side. It is a much easier feat to get Suzy Lit-Girl to repost your blog or your book's review than it is to make it onto Oprah's radar (let alone get a plug). Additionally, those who follow Suzy view her as an authority and listen to her much like an expert, even though, by strict definition, she isn't.

Thirdly, there are far more referent influencers than expert influencers. A lot more. There are a lot more Suzy Lit-Girls to befriend than Oprahs.

*** *Many referent influencers are considered experts in certain subject areas. Pay attention.*

Positional Influencer—is often in the person's inner circle. Friends, family, spouses are all examples of positional influencers. Yes, whether most of us admit it or not, our mothers' opinions still influence us.

Virtually everyone on social media is a positional influencer to someone else. Positional influencers can be very valuable to a writer, especially in certain genres. For instance, I imagine that most 4-year-olds don't drive down to Barnes & Noble, slap down a credit card and buy a stack of kid's books. But moms do. If you happen to write for children, middle grade, teens, or any group that typically would not be the purchaser of the book, then you must target the positional influencers or risk losing a huge percentage of your potential consumers.

This goes back to profiling the reader as part of your social media campaign. One would also be wise to profile the purchaser.

Ideally, you will recruit the referent and expert influencers who hold sway over the positional influencers. Recruit SuperCarpool_Mom (referent influencer) and @ParentingMagazine to your side and the moms will listen.

*** *The key to doing social media well, resides in recruiting and mobilizing all types of influencers, particularly the referent and expert influencers.*

At the end of the day, be good to anyone who is being good to you. Networks are hard to build, and we need as much help as we can get from our social community. So if others help "raise your barn," (repost your posts) make sure you pitch in with theirs. It is just good manners.

I might qualify, I advise being kind and reciprocating because it is the right thing to do. But, we do have to deal with reality. We only have so much time. Yes, we need to be good to as many as we can, but we need to be mindful to pay attention to those with greater reach and influence if we hope to have time left over to write great books. We need to learn to work smarter not harder.

Part of working smarter is that we develop the habits of successful people.

Kristen Lamb

Searching for Treasure—The Winner Inside

Many of you reading this aspire to be professional authors, and that is a fantastic goal. Writing can be the best job in the world, but too many beginners glamorize the profession and fail to get the proper emotional preparation before traipsing off to battle. That is a formula to get creamed.

Becoming a professional writer isn't all rainbows and unicorns. Let's face it. Many of us have our basic personality working against us. What do I mean? To put it bluntly, writing is a vortex of flakes. We creative people are not usually known for our self-discipline. I've been there. I don't know about you, but I am a notorious procrastinator. I was once the High Queen of Do-It-Later Land, a sorrowful place of forgotten Post-It Notes, where the roads are paved with shiny good intentions.

What I have observed over the years is that very often, the personalities that are the most creative also tend to be free-spirits who flutter around like fruit flies with severe ADHD high off a case of Red Bull. Now, we are great at being creative, but unless it's channeled and focused, creativity just looks like that kid who likes to run head-first into a wall over and over while giggling. Thus, it is easy to see why people might roll their eyes the day we announce we want to be a writer.

Writing is a very emotional business, and to write well, we must reach into the deepest parts of our being…and then place them out for public display. After running countless critique groups and helping hundreds of writers, I will share some advice that will help you reach your dreams. All the craft classes and social media efforts in the world will not benefit you if your heart and mind aren't in the correct place.

Persistence Can Look a lot like Stupid

Oh, Twitter. It is so fun to watch all these writing quotes float by. One of the favorites of the newbie writer (Yes, it was mine too) is,

41

"You know what you call the writer who never gives up? Published." I have no idea who said that, and it doesn't matter anyway. Don't get me wrong, it is a great quote. But, it really kind of needs a caveat, because persistence can look a lot like stupid.

My goal can be to climb Mt. Everest, but if I am on Mt. Shasta then I am not persistent, I am a moron.

You are on the wrong mountain!

Can't hear you! I'm climbing! Never give up!

But you are on the wrong mountain, you idiot!

What? You're just a dream-stealer! My motivational coach said you would try to stop me! I'm climbing! Never give up!

I teach at a lot of conferences, and every year I see the same writers shopping the same novel that has been rejected time and time and time again. These writers show year after year spending good money, believing that they just haven't found the right agent who will see the beauty in their vampire-mystery-romance-YA-horror-memoir. It is as if they are stuck in a feedback loop. They can't move on until this book gets an agent. They believe that if they don't get an agent for this book, then they are a failure. No!

I have been there. I shopped my first novel for three years then woke up one day and realized I was swimming against the current carrying a corpse. When you make a decision to become a writer, you will be swimming against the current. People are fascinated by people who dare to dream and do great things. But...deep down, while they admire them, they also resent them.

Do not expect your family to embrace your decision. In fact, as I warned you earlier, expect them to believe your writing group is really a cult. So expect to be swimming upstream, which is a heck of a lot harder to do carrying dead weight. If your book is being rejected time and time and time again, move on. Maybe you will grow enough to fix that first novel at a later time. Or, maybe you will take it for what it is...a learning experience. Always be moving forward.

Persistence is a noble trait; tunnel-vision is not.

Be persistent. Read more books on the craft. Sign up for workshops. Read...a lot. Be persistent the right way and the payoff will eventually come.

Learn to Fail Forward

One of the biggest frustrations I have with writers is their attitude toward failure. I think we like being tragic. Goes with our artsy side.

Hand over the beret. Give. This is for your own good.

Learn to have a healthy relationship with failure. One of my favorite books is *Failing Forward* by John Maxwell. I highly recommend it to everyone. This book changed my life.

I used to have constant panic attacks. I was absolutely paralyzed by fear. All I could see was what I hadn't accomplished. I magnified my failures and minimized my progress. Instead of looking forward, I was always looking over my shoulder to the past, crying over the broken dreams and what ifs? That is a load of crap.

Want to know the difference between winners and losers? There are 2 critical differences.

1.   Winners have a healthy relationship with failure.

Losers cry and whine and self-flagellate when they fail to meet the mark. Their focus is always on failure, so that's where they stay. Winners, however, look at failure as a stepping stone. They land on their tush and scratch their head and ask critical questions.

Why didn't this work?

What went wrong?

At what point did my plan go south?

What can I do differently next time?

Do I need to adjust my goals?

All through the month of November (which is National Novel Writing Month) I keep my eyes on the #nanowrimo hash tag column. For those of you unfamiliar with Twitter, a # symbol will put you in a group bound by that topic. Time after time I have wanted to scream as writers posted crap like this:

My goal was 1000 words today. Only wrote 300. #nanowrimo #epicfail

I saw that stupid #epicfail over and over and over. Now how do you think the Epic Fail group fared for National Novel Writing Month?

But, I also saw tweets like this:

My goal was 1000. Only made 500. Hey, 500 more than I had. Will start earlier tomorrow. #nanowrimo

Which writer will have a better chance at success?

Inspirational speaker Joyce Meyer has a great quote that has become a cornerstone in my thinking: **Where the mind goes, the man follows.**

Kristen Lamb

If our mind is always on our failure and where we blew it, then that is where we will go. But here is the thing, we are in control. We are the boss. Whether we are writing books or blogging, a positive attitude is paramount if we hope to endure long enough to reap rewards.

I'm going to give you a great tactic to keep your mind on the positive. I want you to picture a monster crouched in your soul. Every time you beat yourself up, call yourself names, whine about how life isn't fair…you feed it. As you feed this monster, he grows larger and larger and hungrier and more demanding.

How do you kill him? You can't. We are human and he is a part of us. We can't kill him, but we sure as hell can weaken him. How?

We starve him.

Every time you go to open your mouth and gripe about some way you failed to make the mark, stop yourself. Take a breath and rephrase in the positive.

I didn't make my goal of 1000 words….BUT I did write 300 and that is 300 words in the right direction. I only wrote one blog today, but that is one more than I had when I woke up. Every day I am getting better and better. I'm not where I want to be, but I am not where I was.

Starve that monster in your soul and he will get skinnier and smaller and weaker. Eventually, he will be starved long enough that he will lose his appetite, and you will be a happier, more optimistic person for it.

2.   Winners have an internal locus of control.

Your locus of focus is very important. People with an external locus of focus believe other people or things hold all the power to their lives.

If my family would just take me seriously, then I know I would write more.

If I just had a better computer, then I'd write more.

If I just had quiet time, then I would be more productive.

IF we want to be winners, our goal is to maintain an internal locus of focus. We are in control of all things. We cannot control others. We cannot control events. The only thing under our power is our attitude and how we react to other people, events, and circumstances.

Well, my family thinks I'm a nut. I hope that changes. The only thing I can do is work hard and maybe one day my work ethic and

44

commitment will change their opinions.

This old laptop crashes every other time I use it. What can I do to get a new one? In the meantime, maybe I can borrow one, or go to the library, or even write long-hand. It isn't ideal, but Shakespeare didn't have a Mac. I can do this.

I know I need quiet time to be productive. Can I stay up later? Get up earlier? Either I need to actively seek quiet time, or I will just have to be happy with a lower level of productivity. At least I am being fruitful with my time.

Be the captain of your own ship; the master of your soul (Invictus). No one is control of your destiny but you, and you have a lot more power than you believe.

Face Your Fears

I owe my friend and mentor Bob Mayer a lot, but the biggest lesson he taught me was to learn to face my fear. Do what is counterintuitive. I know that if I start feeling a flutter in my gut, then I am likely on the right path. The best writing in you lies behind your greatest fears. Think of it this way. Just expect a dragon to be guarding the cavern of treasure. In fact, the bigger the treasure, the bigger the beast standing sentinel.

Courage is not being without fear. Courage is feeling fear, but then doing it anyway. Only idiots and sociopaths are devoid of fear. Fear is your friend. Fear is like a water witch guiding you to your greatest reservoirs of creativity and strength. When you feel fear, keep going. Likely you're onto something. No one ever accomplished anything great staying in the comfort zone.

For many of you, the thought of blogging is enough to make you want to hide in your room and lock the door. I totally understand. Blogging makes us vulnerable. It means putting ourselves out there for criticism. Blogging can be scary, but it can also be the most rewarding experience you will ever have. I was terrified when I first started blogging. That's one of the biggest reasons I started teaching this stuff. I wanted you to know that you are not alone, and that you are capable of far more than you believe.

I hope you feel fired up, and that you're ready to take on that list of goals. I'll be here to help you every step of the way. So what are your biggest challenges? Biggest fears? Write them down. Toss them out there. Sometimes the monster in the closet is only a coat when you turn the light on.

Speaking of monsters, let's shift gears again. I wouldn't be doing my job if we didn't discuss how to avoid some real monsters, the predators lurking on the web.

5 Ways to Stay Safe on Social Media

Time to address a very important topic. Operational security. What is operational security? In a nutshell? Understand your enemy and deny him access.

When it comes to social media, I see many writers on both extremes of the spectrum. On one end of the spectrum is the writer who creates an entirely new identity. Let's call her **Paranoid Peggy**. She doesn't want her friends or family to know about her writing, so she generally does one of two things.

One approach is that Paranoid Peggy creates fan pages and Twitter accounts using cutesy monikers and an avatar. She feels that once she gets published then she can let people know she is a writer. This approach very often is driven by fear of failure and will destroy a platform.

But Paranoid Peggy also is known to take a second approach. She uses a picture (maybe) but she builds all her social media pages completely separate from her personal life and under a pen name. This is an entirely acceptable approach, but not a wise one. This approach will cost Peggy a lot of duplicated effort that will cut into her writing time.

Paranoid Peggy also frequently has another behavior that can be harmful to building her platform. This type of writer often doesn't divulge anything personal and social media is all about business. The problem with this approach is that social media is, above all else…social. Take this approach and a writer risks being perceived as little better than a spam bot.

Tweeting or posting about mundane things like, "My dog ate my shoes" is important. Now if that is all you tweet about then you have a problem. But, posting about mundane occurrences is like mentioning the weather. It makes it easy for people to approach you and strike up a conversation. Conversations are the foundation of relationships, and relationships lead to relationship sales, which is why we writers are here in the first place.

My nature, believe it or not, is to be a Paranoid Peggy. I even hate those little stickers on the back of mini-vans. You know what I am talking about. The stick figures? Mom, Dad, three kids and a dog. So a robber knows exactly how many people he has to subdue when he breaks into the house. Oh, and hamburger full of sleeping pills for the dog. See? I told you I could be dark.

Anyway….

Time to look at the other side of the spectrum…the **Loosey-Goosey Lucy**. On social media it is very easy to get a false sense of security. I see information all the time posted on Facebook and Twitter that predators would looooove to get their grubby too-good-to-work-like-the-rest-of-us-hands on. So, some tips to keep you social, yet safe.

1.   Just because there is a box does not mean you are obligated to fill it out.

Facebook in particular collects a lot of personal information with the intent of making social media more enjoyable. Okay, fair enough. But we have to be prudent what we put out there and cannot blindly trust that Facebook is above being hacked or phished. Facebook recently found itself in hot water for selling private information to retailers for the purposes of direct marketing. So, let's just say Facebook is fallible.

Oh, but Kristen, we can set the security protocols. Yep, and you are fallible, too. All it takes is one mistake and suddenly your cell number and address are out to God only knows who. I know Facebook means well when it provides you little boxes for all your e-mail addresses and home address and cell number. Just leave them blank. The Facebook police will not show up and make you do detention because you didn't finish your social media homework. If someone really needs your cell number they can message you and ask like a normal person.

2.   NEVER EVER UNDER ANY CIRCUMSTANCE PUT YOUR BIRTHDAY…. EVER!

Yes, I get really picky about this one. My first job as a writer was to write manuals for a lab that did Questioned Document Analysis. Basically they analyzed handwriting and used all kinds of gadgets to detect forgery. It is shocking how easy it is for someone to steal an identity.

What is even more shocking is how easy it is for us to prevent them from stealing our identities. Thieves love to get a hold of birthdays. And I know it is kind of a bummer because now you might not get as much digital birthday cake on your Wall, but tough cookies. If people are really your friends they will know your birthday. It stuns me how many Facebook pages I see with the person's full name and the day, month, and year right up under the picture.

Please understand; these are easy mistakes to make. Most of us are not evil identity thieves and thus it isn't natural for us to think like one. Don't feel dumb if you have to put down this book to go take down your birthday. I have made all the mistakes, too.

3.   Avoid specific information.

On all of my sites, you will see that I live in Dallas, TX or in DFW. I actually live in one of the satellite communities, but DFW is close enough for government work. Never post pictures of your home with identifiable landmarks or addresses. I have posted pictures of my garden, but I make sure that there is nothing in the image that could help some weirdo locate my actual home.

4.   Have a separate page for personal stuff.

Do you have to do this? No, but it does make life easier. Sometimes you just want to talk politics and about the kids and your time at church or synagogue or Wicca Camp without it adversely affecting your platform. Facebook is not going to mind you having more than one page so long as they are active and you are using them. Facebook just frowns on having lots and lots of pages that people are squatting on the name/domain without interacting in the community. I have a separate page under my married name, and if people want to see family pictures, they have to know me. This is the page where I talk to all of my friends from grade school and third cousins and writers who are my personal friends. All the security protocols are set to default to the strictest setting so I don't have to worry that pictures of my family Christmas are being looked at by everyone on the Internet.

5.   Never tweet or post a status update announcing you or your home is vulnerable.

If you followed the above rules, this becomes less critical, but it still is just a bad idea to feed predators real-time intel. I see friends announce things all the time like, "Yay! We are finally leaving for Florida for a week. Glad to be on the way to the airport!" Um, they just told every potential burglar that they will be gone, how long they will be gone, and that their house is potentially unattended. I tend to get paranoid on this point. I will announce activities...but only retrospectively. For example, don't post, "Off to the gym." Rather, post something like, "Whew! Just got home from the gym. I feel so much better." This way, you can get the benefit of the personal interactions without opening your home to potential threats.

Now that I have you all too scared to use social media, calm down. These rules are just common sense. Paranoid Peggy and Loosey-Goosey Lucy are two extremes that we want to avoid so we can make our social media time effective for building our platform. Social media is a friendly place, and it can be easy to let our guard down. It is imperative that we be social and friendly, but by employing a few checks, we can do so in a way that is prudent and safe.

Okay, all of you know how to stay safe. We are going to move on and discuss a critical concept in social media. Everything hinges on creating a brand. This is another way we work smarter, not harder.

More than an Author? How to Become a Household Name—Branding 101

Want to become more than just an author? Do you want to be an icon, a household name like Stephen King or Nora Roberts? Do you want your name to sell your books so you don't have to? Then you must understand branding. Branding is vital to any writer who wants to have a career in publishing, yet it often amazes me how many writers don't understand the process. And that is okay in the beginning. I get it. You are writers, not Madison Avenue. But *tempus fugit*—time is fleeting. The learning curve these days is steep for sure. I am here to show you that, if you grasp branding properly, every marketing effort, every social media endeavor will be magnified exponentially...leaving you more time to write great books.

Writers are wise to respect what lies ahead. Until we are in the big leagues, we will be expected to do a lion's share of our own marketing. I met Amy Tan last year. Ms. Tan gets a pass since she's a household name, and her books come with Cliff's Notes. Until we get that big, we need to expect a lot of work. But I don't know about you. I happen to prefer working smart over working hard any day of the week.

Publishing is more competitive than ever. Agencies want to see strong writing, but they are now also expecting writers to be able to demonstrate an existing platform that can translate into book sales. This is one of the many reasons that the earlier you begin building a platform, the better. Yes, you unpubbed writers out there. Start now.

To make matters complicated, there are a lot of well-meaning social media folk happy to lend their services on-line and at conferences. Yet, many of these social media experts fail to appreciate that writers are different. Many practices that work great in Corporate America break down when used to brand an author. This is what makes my books and blogs different. I have been a writer and editor for going on ten years and appreciate the unique paradigm an author faces. Your brand will be your foundation, and no matter what anyone says, you are the brand.

This is the largest stumbling block for many writers and even social media folk. Our books are not the brand...we are. When most people hear Amy Tan, they instantly think *Joy Luck Club*. Yet, there isn't a week that goes by that I don't see some well-intended marketing person advising writers to buy domains with the name of their books or have blogs or Twitter accounts from the perspectives of characters. Want the truth? None of that serves to build your brand as an author, and it is a formula to go crazy and spread yourself so thinly that you don't have time left over to produce the product...quality books.

Branding the title of your book, whether published or unpublished, is a bad idea.

Why do so many marketing folk assume writers need to brand a book? Well, plainly put, it is a really easy mistake to make, because in the traditional business world, these tactics work. Since these guys are marketing experts they frequently don't understand how publishing works. Thus, they try to give writers the tools that kick butt in business, unaware that they are doing more harm than good. I have even been put in tight spots at conferences because I was teaching contrary to the other social media class down the hall. But that's okay. We are here to learn.

Why is branding the title of your book a bad idea?

Mainstream social media folk think in business terms. They think, well if I am a business owner, I don't promote my name, I promote my business. This tactic works great in Corporate America. In business, if I decide to open up a small business, I can go file for a DBA. I know the name of my business. Say I want to open a dog grooming shop and call it *Paw-parazzi*. Once I have the green light on the name and the appropriate licenses then I know it is a good idea to go buy that domain for a web page. I also know I need a logo and to send out mailers and e-mails and flyers and Facebook fan pages all with *Paw-parazzi*. Why? Because I want *Paw-parazzi* to be the name that comes to mind when anyone needs their pooch shampooed. *Paw-parazzi* is THE place to give your doggie the treatment she deserves (brand).

Unless *Paw-parazzi* goes bankrupt, or I sell the shop, or for some reason decide to close the business (one too many dog bites), I know I own the rights to use the name *Paw-parazzi*. Thus I will promote this name (brand) until I retire, die, sell or go under.

As a writer, it is easy to assume that the book is the product. So, logically, I will want to begin building a platform and promoting my book. Ah, here's the tar baby, though.

Unless you self-publish, you will have little to no control over the title. For business reasons, a publishing company reserves the right to change the title at any time, right up to the minute before the book goes to print. Generally the decision to change a title is in the author's best interests. Publishing houses do not make money unless we writers sell lots and lots of books. Thus, if they change the title, there is a strategic reason for doing so.

I see many unpublished writers running out and buying domains and building web sites for unpublished works. You certainly have the right spirit (ROCK ON!), but not the correct focus. If the title of your book changes before the book goes to print, that is a heck of a lot of work and money down the tubes.

And say the title of your book doesn't change. If you want to be a career author, then it stands to reason that you will write more than one book. Now you are back at square one. Are you really motivated enough to build separate platforms for every single title you write? There wouldn't be any time left over to write more books. Think about my earlier example of Amy Tan. She wasn't always a household name. Do you think it would have been a wise use of her time to build web sites and social media pages for *Joy Luck Club*, *The Bonesetter's Daughter*, *Hundred Secret Senses*, *Kitchen God's Wife*...you get the point. She probably wouldn't have had time to write all of these. She would have been too busy marketing.

But what about self-published authors?

Recently I had a rather heated Twitter discussion with a person teaching social media marketing to writers. She asserted that if an author was self-published, then she thought it was critical to brand the title of the book. Fair enough. Self-publishing is certainly an option and a great way to break into a larger market. But we still need to look at long-term goals. If you are self-publishing with hopes it will ignite a career as an author, you still need to brand your name. Why? Well, let's look at this logically.

A lot of self-published authors are going this route in hopes of demonstrating high enough sales to attract the attention of a larger publisher. So say you happen to be successful and sell a good number of books.

NY comes calling. If you branded the title of your book and not your name, then you are back in the same conundrum. The publisher reserves the right to change the title. Also, if you want to be a career author and write more than that one book, then you are back at square one for the next book and the next and the next.

Agents and editors want to see great books, and they really get excited when those books come tethered to people who understood how to correctly brand. So why aren't more writers branding correctly? Misinformation accounts for a lot, but fear accounts for more.

Most of the time it is fear that keeps us from using our name. Because we fear failure, rejection, criticism, etc. we hide behind clever monikers, or we emotionally distance behind branding the title of a book. I say, name it and claim it. It is scary, but vital. If I told you today that I could hit you with super-duper writer magic dust and guarantee that you would be a huge success, would you still want a moniker or a book title as your brand? Stephen King, Stephenie Meyer, Amy Tan, Nora Roberts, James Rollins, Tom Clancy, Mary Higgins Clark are all very proud to use their names. If we want to one day be like them then we need to act like them.

Speaking of acting like winners. Setting goals and being able to pursue them with single-minded determination is a key factor in success. This next selection is to train you to think like elite race car drivers...*oooooooohhh*. Cool, I know.

Focus on the Goal

Years ago, when I first became a writer I befriended a gentleman, James Dunne, who worked for Ferrari. I was writing a novel set in Monte Carlo and wanted to know all I could about the Formula One and the cars, people, etc. I also attended the first NASCAR races in DFW and became friends with members of Dale Earnhardt Sr.'s pit crew to get an inside perspective on car racing. It was a tremendous experience. The book is in a drawer, but the lessons were forever. I took away a maxim that has affected how I approach life and people, and today I will share it with you guys.

Race car drivers not only have to go top speed (duh) but the largest part of winning is staying in the race. Drivers stay in the race if they can avoid colliding with other cars and keep from hitting the wall. Rocket science here, right? Bear with me. When race car drivers train, they are taught to keep their eyes where they want to go. Why? Because where the eyes go, the car follows. Thus, they are instructed that, to avoid hitting the wall, never look at the wall. Or more accurately: To avoid hitting the wall, focus on the finish line.

Race car drivers always keep their eyes on the straightaway and on the finish line. This was a life-changing lesson for me. Where the mind goes the man follows. Race car drivers aren't foolish. They know the wall is there. Yet, they understand that staring at it is not going to do anything positive for getting them closer to the checkered flags.

In life, we must do all we can to ignore the walls and keep our eyes on the prize. This has a lot to do with positive thinking, which beats being negative any day of the week. Our thought life is vitally important to our attitude, and our attitude is the most vital component of how we treat ourselves and others. How do we avoid walls? We watch two things—our focus and our mouth.

Watching Our Focus

For years I volunteered teaching children in a Christian after school program. We generally inherited most of the problem kids because no one else wanted them around. These kids hit and kicked and had no concept of self control. I noticed that when we corrected them or chastised them for a certain behavior, we could soon expect more of it...a LOT more. So we volunteers decided to change our approach with these little "scoundrels."

Even though it made me want to pull out my hair, I began ignoring most of their acting out. Yet, when they settled down and were quiet, I offered heaping praise. When they played nicely with other kids, I made a big production of what great kiddos they were. It wasn't long until most of these kids were happy, smiling, and well-behaved. They craved attention. All I did was lavish attention for better behavior.

The strange thing was that a few of them didn't change. Some of the kids still acted up. They didn't change, but I did. I could still care for them and enjoy them because I focused on the good they had to offer.

Other people always have "walls" and I make a deliberate act to ignore them. It doesn't do me or other people any good to focus on weakness or where they fall short, because we all fall short. I find that if I focus on how someone is always late or disorganized or negative, pretty soon it colors how I treat that person. Yet, I notice that if I can look for the good, then eventually I get to the point where I don't even see the bad. It isn't that their "wall" isn't there; it just isn't my sole focus.

This is one of the reasons it is crucial to focus on the progress we make on social media. When we get negative comments on our blog, it is very easy to fall into depression by focusing on what one person hated about our post. If we aren't careful, it can have us revamping the entire format or changing our blogging voice, when there might not be anything wrong. Take all criticism into account and make necessary changes, but, beyond that? *Fugettabouit*, as Bob Mayer would say.

We must focus on the positive when it comes to our social media approach, but the same goes for how we treat ourselves in general. I know if I pay undue attention to my flaws, I soon can expect those flaws to get bigger, which leads to my next point....

Watching Our Mouths

Did you know that the subconscious brain cannot tell the difference between truth and lie? Even if we give it wrong information, the subconscious brain will accept it as true. Psychiatrists call this conditioning. Christians say that, out of your mouth you speak life and death; choose life. Both schools imply we have a choice.

If I say, "Today is going to be so horrible." Guess what? Often it is. Why? I spoke it and deemed it so. Thus, instead of noticing the good things that happen, my eyes will be fixed on "walls" all day long because I have instructed them to do so. I will look for every little thing that doesn't go my way to affirm the belief I have stuck in my head... "Today is going to be horrible."

"Oh I just know I am going to be late for that meeting." Hmmm. Suddenly I cannot find my keys, my bag, my purse, my butt.

Another point. Did you know that the human brain also has this weird way of chopping off conditionals, and it only begins to listen at the first active verb? This is why negative goals can submarine our best efforts.

I say: Don't forget your folder.
Brain hears: Forget your folder.
I say: Don't overeat tonight at dinner.
Brain hears: Overeat at dinner.
I say: Under no certain circumstances will you bait to that woman at the board meeting.
Brain hears: Bait to that woman at the board meeting.
I say: Now make sure you don't lose that business card.
Brain hears: Lose that business card.

If you tell a writer, "The pitch session isn't the end of the world. Don't panic." I guarantee you she hears, "Pitch session. End of the world. Panic."

If you tweet, "Don't forget my book signing tomorrow" then just go ahead and expect low attendance.

How we speak is critical. I have found that phrasing things in the positive makes a remarkable difference. When I come in the door, I say, "Now remember your keys are here." When I am going to a restaurant that I know can make me eat until I pop, I say, "I am going to only eat until I am full." When I wake up in the morning I say, "I am going to have a great day." When I am staring down the barrel of having to face a horrible, negative person, I tell myself, "I am going to be calm and maintain my peace." Is this some kind of magic charm? No. But I do find this approach mitigates the negative. I might find that my temper flares at that person who feels the need to sabotage a committee meeting, but it isn't as bad as if I had told myself, "If such-and-such says one word, I am going to give her what-for."

This approach also works with others. I find that when I tell my husband, "Remember to pick up your slacks from the cleaners" that my odds are better that he will come home with his dry cleaning.

When I tell my young nephews, "I just know you two are going to make me look good when everyone sees how well you behave." Most of the time, they do.

One of my favorite quotes is from Dale Carnegie. He said, "The ideas I stand for are not mine. I borrowed them from Socrates. I swiped them from Chesterfield. I stole them from Jesus. And I put them in a book. If you don't like their rules, whose would you use?"

We have a choice with our attitude, and we have a choice what rules govern how we see others and ourselves. Our focus becomes critical when we are plugged into a digital community of thousands, or even millions. Positive people will enjoy far greater success in life as well as social media.

If the most skilled racecar drivers in the world know to focus on the goal line, and top athletes know to focus on winning, and successful entrepreneurs know to focus on possibility, and successful couples know to focus on love, then we can take a lesson from that. If we want what they have, adopting their habits and attitude is a darn good start. In fact, blogging is a wonderful way to practice this life habit. People love feeling good, and a positive attitude is a key ingredient for a hit blog that connects with others in a meaningful way.

Okay, so now you are focused and ready to be winners. Maybe you are all psyched up and revved to start building your social media empire. Ah, but you don't know what name to use. You have a pen name for every short story you've ever written and your own name just isn't all that memorable and what if your mother finds out you wrote about her favorite sister who was really a circus midget and…

It's all right. I am here to help.

Pen Names are a High-Maintenance Love Affair

There are few things more romantic than the allure of the *nom de plume*. Yet, as writer and a social media expert, I think they are a total time suck and often not worth the trouble. Oh, don't start whining. Don't you think I would have like to have been something a tad more glamorous than Kristen Lamb? When I was 5 my father convinced me that he had legally changed my name to *Mary Hannah*. Get it? *Mary Hannah Lamb?* Yeah, I didn't find it funny either.

Pen names are extra work and they are old paradigm. Before you disagree, let me explain. I actually am on your side.

Let me remind you. Novelists, historically, have had a staggering failure rate. It was actually statistically EASIER to be elected to congress than to make the NY Times best-seller list.

Why? Because writers only had control over the book. Marketing and platform was handled by other people.

Note: I use the term "handled" very loosely, because, even now, if you aren't a heavy hitter, you can expect little to no marketing support. Is it because NY is evil and sitting up all night thinking of ways to sabotage the dreams of new writers? No. They are a business and have overhead and payroll. New writers are an untested commodity, thus money, time and effort gets sunk into proven players. Makes total business sense.

Unless you're the new kid.

But, until now novelists had almost zero control over building a platform of people who knew them and supported them even before the book went to print. These days? Totally different story. There are unagented self-published writers now becoming millionaires because of their **platform**.

In the old days, an author had one way to build a platform—fan love for their books.

Ah, but there is the sticky wicket. If we write a book and no one knows about it, then it is likely to fail because no one knew about it. So the only way to help a book succeed is to have fans, but if no one knows about our books, how do we get fans?

It's kind of like we need experience to get a job, but if we don't get a job, how can we get experience? We need credit to get a credit card but how do we get credit if no one will give us a credit card?

Social media has changed everything. Our following now supports US. People liked and supported Kristen Lamb before I ever even had a finished book (THANKS!). Now I have fans of me *and* my book. How? I built a social media platform.

Now, unlike writers in the past, I do have control over writing a darn good book **and** building a platform. It is double the work, but now I actually exercise some control over my future. It is already double the work, why make even more?

When I began seriously writing, I had a full-time job and I cared for my mother. Then, I had to find time to write, too. I am sure some of you can relate. We already have a full-time day job and kids and pets and needy houseplants, why balance multiple identities when you don't have to? Why make the marketing side an even BIGGER chore?

Let's look into traditional reasons to have a pen name, and why, most of the time, they are no longer valid.

Privacy—Okay, privacy is an illusion. Unless you only use cash and live as a wandering hobo on the fringes of society eating out of trash cans in darkened alleys, there is no such thing. Everything is electronic. That grocery store card on your keychain that saves you money is recording everything you buy and how often. We are on camera everywhere we go. Nothing about our life is private . . . period. Believing that a pen name is somehow going to give us this magical anonymity is like thinking that hiding under a blanket makes us invisible.

If we want to build an entirely new identity for marketing purposes, that is great. But we cannot suffer any illusions that we can hide. It is a pen name, not witness protection. Yes, historically, the *nom de plume* was a safe haven. That is ancient history.

An example:

Say I write kid's books under one name and hardcore bondage erotica under a pen name. Stop laughing.

All it takes is someone taking my picture at an event or a book signing then posting that on their Facebook page for everything to crumble. Someone surfing the web recognizes me as the same lady who read her new kid's book at the mall.

Now I potentially have a huge problem. I tried to use my pen name to *hide* what I was doing.

I have friends who write erotica, and they are fun and wild and carefree, and often like hanging around a giggly pajama party. But these women feel very confident in their work and their sexuality, and, if they are using a pen name, it is to make their writing sell more copies *because their name sounds sexier*. Their motivation is not to hide from the world what they are doing.

BIG difference.

Any ten-year-old with basic computer skills can find out our real name. As search engines get faster and better and more and more people are contributing content? The problem only grows larger. Yes, for now, pen names offer a thin veneer of privacy, but it is growing thinner by the day. It is a Brave New World. There are blessings, but they come at a price. Will a pen name offer a degree of privacy? Sure. Just like locking the screen door to our house will keep most visitors from waltzing in our front door. A pen name is an extra layer that will keep out most people, but not the highly motivated. We just have to be realistic of the protection it offers.

People at work will find out—This is the same scenario. Privacy is an illusion. The good news is that most normal people don't spend their free time Googling coworkers to see what they are up to when they leave the employee parking lot. That's just weird . . . and kind of creepy.

Just write. If you become a best-selling author you won't be working there anymore anyway. Why care?

I have a difficult last name—On social media we get to see people's names over and over and over. We don't have to be able to pronounce your last name in order to recognize it. In fact, that name you have hated since grade school actually can help you stand apart from all the other writers. Don't take my word for it; ask Janet Evanovich.

If my name is Inga Skjold, all someone needs to remember is my name begins with "Skj..." and the search engines will deliver me right to their page.

Google has red slanty letters to correct people who misspell your name. Go type in, "Author Janet Ewanoviche" and see what happens. Google will be right there with red slanty letters asking "*Did you mean Author Janet Evanovich?*"

My name is boring— Okay, our name is only half of the brand. NAME + CONTENT = BRAND.

Stephen King was a boring name shared by thousands of other young men. Then, the name was associated *so many times* with horror writing that the name *Stephen King* is now synonymous with horror, and I really feel sorry for King's male peers who share his name.

Our name only sells books because people *recognize* it. How many of you have ever said, "Wow, that author has a really snazzy name. I think I will buy her book"? We buy books because the *title of the book* sounds cool or the *story* sounds interesting. Dan Brown, Sandra Brown, Stephen King are not terribly exotic names.

The pen name is not the place to be glamorous. Earning fat royalty checks that let us go spend a weekend at a spa is the real place to get glamorous. If we don't have time left over to write great books, then who cares what our name is?

I write more than one genre—For now? Yes, that might be necessary. My opinion? This practice is going extinct and will be dead before the end of the decade. I give it five years max.

Historically, publishing houses made authors use different names if they switched genre. Why? Because the only platform a novelist could grow was a platform of people who loved the writer's **books**.

We were trapped under a traditional marketing paradigm. The general public wasn't on-line interacting real time with their favorite authors. We needed multiple names to keep readers from getting confused.

I have a confession. Are you sitting down? I write thrillers, too. How many of you just had your brains explode? No one? Did it rip the fabric of your reality that I do *more than one thing*?

This is the first time in history that authors had control over their platform. ONE NAME. If you must have a pen name, build it under the umbrella of YOUR NAME.

New York Times Best-Selling Author Bob Mayer has his books listed on his site. We get that Bob Mayer writes thrillers, sci-fi, romance, NF, and now historical fiction . . . and yet we live to tell the tale.

If you want sci-fi, check out Bob Mayer *as* Robert Doherty. Still alive? Good. See how easy that was?

If you build your platform using your own name, and your agent wants you to have a pen name? No problem. Just keep business as usual then mention in your blogs and tweets, "Oh and soon my romance under my pen name FiFi Fakename will be available for sale. I'll let you know when." *Notice you don't have to scurry off and build an entirely new platform with an entirely new identity.*

I am afraid of failure—Join the club! Some of you want to wait until the writing is successful to let friends and family know about the other half of your life. But it is coming at the cost of you spreading yourself too thinly to be effective.

Dreams come with risk. We don't get a pass on risking failure. We all risk that. I have failed many, many times, and I have learned to take my lumps, laugh it off and keep going. Failure is part of life, and it is a core ingredient of the successful life. If we are spending so much time hedging against a fall, then we are planning for failure. Our focus is in the wrong spot. Focus on success. Reread the last chapter.

When we use the name that all our friends and family, coworkers and people who knew us in school remember, we get an added advantage of activating our intimate networks. I have people who barely spoke to me in high school who are now some of my biggest cheerleaders. They are excited to get to support a writer they *know.*

Never underestimate the power of those close connections. The same family members rolling their eyes at you now will be the first to buy a book and tell all their friends and coworkers.

My Great Aunt Iris who is almost 98 years old was so proud of herself for reading my book, and she brags about me to everyone she knows. This is a woman who began life in a horse-drawn carriage who is now, almost a century later, reading a book about Twitter. But she loves me and wants to support me and she bought her own copy of my book, even though she is not a writer, has never used a computer, and has severe macular degeneration and can barely see. The point of this story? There are probably some unlikely friends and family who will be there to help you succeed. Don't so quickly count them out.

And, as a quick note, if you want to use a pen name simply

because you are using family members or close connections as character templates, and you are worried they will find out and sue? Here's some good news. Most of them will not recognize themselves in your work. People don't see their flaws the way others do. Why do you think we spend years in therapy? Some of us need to spend $150 per hour for half a decade to see that we might actually have something to do with our own problems. Duh. So relax. These individuals will likely read your book and say, "Boy that Suzy character was an awful and difficult woman. What a manipulator. She reminds me of such-and-such...."

...and you can just smile.

I actually heard attorney and literary agent Paul Levine address this point. He said that, in order for someone to sue a writer for libel, there is a tremendous burden of proof on their part. The plaintiff must prove that anyone reading our work, without a doubt, would know our character was based off of them, and that, as a result, their reputations have suffered irreparably. Tough to prove.

So if you are adopting a pen name because you are worried the evil secretary at work whom you are using as your villain will sue? Just change up the character enough to squash any court argument...and go ahead and use your real name. If you are really worried, contact Paul and hire him to look at your work just to make sure.

Being a successful writer is hard, and becoming a career author is getting harder by the day. Why make it any harder? Your close networks are going to be your first fans. Your family will be lined up for a copy of your first published book, regardless of whether they know postmodern literature from a comic book. They likely will also tell all their friends, family and coworkers about your book.

I hope you can see by now that we really cannot "hide" in a pen name anyway. With the Internet and so much free information flying around, if someone is truly motivated to figure out the person behind the pen name...they likely can. You really cannot disappear if that's the motivation.

Am I against pen names? Yes. Sorry. As a social media expert, I have to say that, for the most part, pen names are a total time suck. Am I *always* against pen names? No. But I do advise that you take a moment and ask some important questions first. If I the magic genie could wave a wand and GUARANTEE that in three years you would be an international success, would you still want the pen name? If the answer is yes, then go for it and make sure you get a copy of WANA so you know how to tackle building a platform for your pen name without making yourself crazier than necessary.

Most of us will fare best by sticking with our real names. Sigh. Yes, Kristen Lamb is not exactly a glamorous name, but it is easy for me and others to remember. In the end, the name is about what can SELL the most books, and less about whether we always wished our parents named us something cooler, like Anastasia or Isabella.

Whether you use a pen name or your given name, there will likely come a time that your career will require you to create a fan page. *Gasp!* I know. It's gonna be okay. I'm here to walk you through a way to build a fan page and maintain your dignity. You might realize you don't need that *nom de plume* after all.

But, say you really, really, really must have a pen name. Okay, this next section will help you keep all your alter egos on a leash, and still make use of your intimate networks.

3 Steps to Fan Page Awesomeness

Time to tackle the ever-mysterious Facebook Fan Page. If you are like me and were born a D&D loving nerd, there have been few opportunities to feel more like a loser than the fan page. If done incorrectly, building a fan page can cause anxiety, heart palpitations, and a recurrence of that nightmare where even though you are 36 and have an advanced degree, your high school counselor shows up to your place of employment to announce that your credits never counted and ergo you never graduated and that you start tenth grade on Monday. EEK!

Trust me. I feel your pain. But, we writers persevere despite because we really, really, really want to be taken seriously...and so we look to the fan page.

The good news is that Facebook has made the fan page a tad easier to endure in that now people can simply "like" us instead of becoming "a fan." I guess the moniker "fan" just implied too much emotional commitment. But now you have no excuse when it comes to taking that professional leap and creating a fan page.

All writers need a fan page. Period. I know there has been a lot of debate about this, but I am right and they are wrong, so there. Seriously. How many of you new writers out there are planning to fail? Like literally. You woke up this morning and went, *Yeah I am so happy about that thousand words I got down on my novel. Too bad no one will read these words until they are packing up my things when I'm DEAD.* What? No one? No takers? How many of you thought, *I just love wasting time. Nothing like watching the months and years of my life slip by with nothing to show for it *cue "Dust in the Wind."**

This was my sarcastic way of saying that all writers, regardless the level, should plan for success. Yes, even the newbie who is still trying to scrape her memory for what a heck a dangling participle actually is…and not giggle like it's eighth grade. Yes, you too. No hiding in the back of the classroom.

All writers need a fan page. Now, when you publish that fan page will be up to you. Why a fan page? Well, among many other advantages we cannot discuss right now.…

- Fan pages can separate your identity from You Normal Person to You the Author.
- Fan pages can help you establish a pen name, should you decide you need one even though I have done all I can to persuade you otherwise.
- Fan pages help others take you seriously as a professional.
- Fan pages will help you manage large numbers of fans in the future with less hassle than a standard FB page.

I go into all of this in far more detail in WANA, so we will just give an overview right now. If you are planning on being published, you must have a fan page. Sorry. Whether we like it or not marketing is part of the job description. I know most of us would rather have brain surgery with a KFC spork than have to self-promote but that's the cold, hard truth. Anyone tell you different and they are lying or selling something.

But the cool thing is that social media is supposed to be, above all else…social. Writers tend to do one of two things when you tell them they need to market. Either they run screaming for the nearest Ben & Jerry's distributor or they turn into that weird third cousin we haven't talked to since she started selling vitamins out of her car. So no hiding and no turning into a SPAM bot. I'm here to help you find the balance.

FB fan pages are just a way of focusing all your writer energy and efforts into one spot and allowing others to support and encourage one area of your life. They will also help brand your name, even if that brand is wide *Your Name Author* until you figure out whether you want to write about vampires or space aliens or wizards. People can begin to associate *Your Name* with *Author*.

When I first started writing, I had no clue what genre I wanted to focus on. Some days, I still don't. But that was no excuse not to begin branding who I was so that when someone went, "Hey, you know that Kristen Lamb chick?" People automatically replied, "Oh, yeah, the writer-chick." That alone was a great start, and way better than, "Kristen Lamb? The chick who had her skirt tucked in her pantyhose?"

There are right ways and wrong ways to do FB fan pages. Do them incorrectly and you could have more personalities than Sybil running around unattended. You could unwittingly make five times the work for yourself and in the end wind up feeling unloved and abandoned when you have five fans…one is your mother who hacked your password to find out your pen name, and the other four are actually spammers, but you didn't have the heart to delete them.

Let's do this the smart way, shall we?

Here are my 3 Steps to Fan Page Awesomeness:

Step #1—Fan pages, even if you use a pen name, should be created off your personal page.

In fact, if you do not yet have a FB page, I recommend starting a personal page first. Think of this page like the traffic cop, where you will direct those members of your network who want to support you as a writer to your fan page.

Go ahead and build your normal FB page. If you already have a FB page, then no need to start over to keep "your identities" separate. We writers have to have time left over to write great books. Writing excellent books is a lot of work that takes a lot of time. Needless duplicated efforts are bad juju.

Step #2—I recommend building your fan page in secret.

When you are building the page, there is a function that will make the page only visible to you the administrator. You have to have 25 "fans" before the fan page name is yours fair and square. In this instance, I recommend publishing the new fan page only long enough to get 25 friends, family and fellow writers to "like" you and then the name is yours for good.

Think of this like house renovations. When the contractors come and knock out counters and remove all your toilets is not the time to have a little soiree. Take time to construct a nice page. Add good content. Blogs, articles, pictures of you at your critique group, You Tube videos of you speaking. Make it look nice for when you are ready to launch.

Step #3—Hit the Golden Three Hundred.

Spend time getting to know people on your regular page. When you hit three hundred (or whatever number makes you feel comfortable) then send out a bulk invite to all of your friends. See, now you will be super glad that you built this baby off your regular page.

Why? Because 300 or more is fishing from a way bigger pond! And, since you have spent time making the fan page look great, it will be far less awkward for people to "like" you.

Once you make your fan page public then feel free to send people directly to your fan page via buttons or Twitter (all explained in WANA). Or, just hang out on the regular page being a normal person. Take advantage of those close networks of family and friends and never discount what great cheerleaders they can be. Interact on the regular page as long as you can. The fan page lacks the two-way communication that you will need, especially early in your career.

But, doing your fan page this way will maximize time, minimize embarrassment and make the best impression. Nothing like a snazzy fan page to get your friends and family to say, "Wow. I guess she really intends to do this thing." And when you do get an agent and a three-book deal, the hard work on your fan page will already be done, so you can focus on writing great novels instead of starting from scratch.

Now that you have a way to build a fan page and still hold your head high, I want to give you food for thought. Many people will tell you that building a social media presence before you finish a book is a waste of time, hubris, or overinflated ego. They couldn't be more wrong, and this next selection explains why.

Your Writing Future—Are You Investing or Gambling?

There are a lot of writers out there who believe they are playing it safe by not building their brand. Don't think I don't see you. You want to wait until you get an agent to begin blogging and building a platform. The idea of using your name or having a fan page makes you uncomfortable, and you have no idea how to promote when you don't even have a finished book. I have some tough news to tell you. You aren't playing it safe at all. You are gambling with your future. You're playing craps, which is high-risk gambling.

It's okay. Breathe. It's a common and easy mistake. I know you are hesitant, and I am here to help you out. We are going to walk you through some guaranteed ways to lay the groundwork for a successful writing career, but first we need to recalibrate your brain. This might sting a little.

Look into my eyes. You are no longer a hobbyist who enjoys writing. You are a professional author, and certain duties go in the job description (yes, even if you don't yet have a finished book).

I am going to let you in on a little secret: you do not have to be published to be considered a professional author. You don't even have to be finished with your novel to be considered a professional author. All you have to do is decide…then do.

You are a professional author the second you proclaim it to be. Now, when you take on certain habits, one day (hopefully in the near future) you will become a successful professional author. We will talk about those habits in a minute.

Brain hurting? Okay. Work with me. Envision you were born to cook. You knew it from the time you were four years old and tried to make scrambled eggs with your mother's waffle iron. You are only happy when you are cooking and creating new dishes. You are also a chef by trade, and since you want to make a living doing what you love, you decide to open your own restaurant.

The day you take out a business loan to open *Le Awesome French Food* you are officially a chef-restaurant-owner. The entire time that *Le Awesome French Food*'s building is under construction, you are still a chef-restaurant-owner. The restaurant doesn't have to be open and serving quiche for you to be a chef-restaurant-owner. BUT, once that restaurant opens, your habits and the work you did ahead of time (*cough* marketing...um, perfecting recipes, not spending the loan money on women and cheap liquor) will determine whether you will be a successful chef-restaurant-owner or just another flopped restaurant idea. Even though cooking is your passion, and the CORE of *Le Awesome French Food*, you will have to do the un-fun things like accounting, promotion, and marketing...until you make enough profit to outsource.

Okay, back to the world of publishing. You are a professional author. Remember that. Write it on a Post-It backwards and stick it to your forehead so you can see this when you go to the bathroom. Kidding! Okay, maybe not.

Building a social media platform before you are published is smart. It is professional. It is far more professional than throwing caution to the wind and hoping luck will make your book soar up the best-selling list. This isn't Vegas. This is your future. Assuming you want a writing career, you need to be smart.

Building a platform isn't ego or hubris, and anyone who tells you that it is, doesn't understand the industry. And it really doesn't matter if you are unpublished. In fact, you have an edge simply because you don't have anything to sell. You will find it easier to be genuine. And yeah, I am really sorry that this is more work to do, but there are a lot of reasons this career isn't for everyone. Just think of it this way. If you work your butt off now, you stand a better shot of having a legion of interns doing the grunt work for you in the future. It's an investment. Wise people invest. Fools gamble.

The largest majority of book sales (roughly 80%) happen via word-of- mouth. This is why only a fraction of writers sell the most books. Brands sell books. People know Stephen King and Stephenie Meyer and Amy Tan and...

Yeah, yeah, yeah, Kristen. You have told us this until we are blue! Brands! Got it! Sheesh!

Maybe some of you, but I can see others, and you aren't too sure. You hide behind cutesy monikers and blog titles and use pseudonyms so you can keep your writing life secret (from all those people who don't know how to use the Internet, because anyone with Google and a half a brain can find you, but I digress…). I am seeing a glazed look and your palms are getting kind of sweaty when I mention the words *fan page*.

Repeat after me. *I am a professional author. I am a professional author. I am a professional author.*

Because here is the bag of dog poo slapped across the face. If we don't stand up and claim professional status then all we are is gaggle of wanna-be hack hobbyists. Either choose the path of the professional, or forget about quitting your day job and just write for fun. You will save a lot of therapy this way.

An agent isn't the end of the game. Getting an agent is one step in a very large chess match. Great, you knocked off one pawn. No shouting "Checkmate!" yet. There is a lot of game to go. Your agent, should you land one, still has to sell that book to a publishing house. That publishing house then needs to sell so many copies of your book. Don't sell enough copies, and it isn't likely a publishing house will gamble on a losing horse twice. (Self-publishing and indie publishing aren't a panacea and require a MUCH larger platform and you guys need this information even MORE…so no loopholes here).

How do you start looking like a wise investment? You build a platform. Your query letter is your business proposal.

Writers are essentially a small business. Sorry to burst the bubble that you can type on your laptop and get an agent and then your biggest concern will be where to buy your mansion—Malibu or Martha's Vineyard? Yep, Santa isn't real either. Sorry. I was bummed, too.

To be successful writers, we must plan for success. We cannot control if vampires are hot or passé. We cannot control if people are reading more or less. We cannot control if e-books will take over and NY will implode in the process. We can control TWO things. Two things, Kiddies.

Product & Platform

This is why I bust my *tuchus* blogging and suffering for you. I have enough suffering to go around. I am a writer, and my mother is from NY. I know all about guilt. Trust me, I am *verklempt* most of the time.

So to recap. We can control product. My Monday blog posts at www.warriorwriters.wordpress.com are to teach you tactics to get better and better at what you do…writing. We can control our product. Join a writing group, read craft books, read magazines, take workshops, and practice. Grow and get better and stronger. You have yet to do your best work. And here is the deal, writing that novel is a very small part of your job as a career author. You cannot write eight hours a day.

Ah, but here is the next point that just gets a bee in my bonnet every time. We can also control building our platform. In fact, with the changing paradigm of publishing…we are responsible for building this platform. NY ain't going to do it for us. A lot of your work (like our chef friend) will be to build your reputation. Look at it this way: social media gives your brain a break, and you can be doing something productive that serves your career.

Agents are taking fewer clients and publishing houses are backing fewer titles. Why? Because they are in the business of making money, so they are playing it safe by banking on known commodities. Who can really blame them? When it comes to taking on new blood, these guys are looking for good bets. Here's a little illustration to make my point.

If given the choice among three unpublished writers, who do you think they will choose?

Creative Caroline wanted to solely focus on the writing. She felt the Internet was a distraction and only blogged every few weeks when she felt especially inspired. Most of her posts were about her own writing journey with little thought given to serving a reading audience. The total hits on her blog are nothing to write home about. Most of her comments are spam, because she forgets to go in and delete those nice comments from the Chinese Aromatherapy Cheap Handbags Cheap Xanax site. There are no comments, so no proof of a vested, reading audience. Caroline feels it is just too confusing to do Twitter, and thinks FB Fan Pages are just tacky. She does have a Facebook page, but the security is locked down so tightly the Pentagon calls her for pointers.

Creative Caroline is a brilliant writer, and her manuscript is excellent, but the only people who know about her as an author or her book are people in her immediate family, friends and writing group. So if every person Caroline knew bought a book, she might sell 200 books (and that is being generous). When Theoretical Agent Googles her name, Caroline is nowhere to be found until page three. And, when Theoretical Agent finally finds Caroline's blog—Mystic Writer Star Dreams—the agent quickly sees that it hasn't been updated since this past summer.

Ouch.

Networking Ned doesn't have time to read books on his craft or even polish his manuscript. He thinks his marketing is so great that it doesn't matter. He spends hours "friending" people on all the major sites. He knows nothing about anyone, but spams them non-stop offering free downloads of his up-and-coming book. He doesn't genuinely interact with anyone on Twitter, he sends auto-tweets…about himself, his blog, and his book. He relies on auto-follow messages instead of taking the time to type a genuine five-word message. Ned has no time to be genuine. He is too busy thinking only of himself. Networking Ned has a heck of a "platform" to put in his query letter, but the agent can tell in ten pages that Ned doesn't know the fundamentals of his craft. The book, to be blunt…sucks.

Prudent Polly was overwhelmed by the publishing industry, but she noted all the e-readers and PDAs and figured that the Internet wasn't going away, so she needed to understand it. She sought out resources to help her use social media effectively, because she read in mega-super-literary-agent Donald Mass's *Writing the Breakout Novel* that marketing dollars didn't make a difference—good writing & word of mouth sold the most books. Word of mouth and good writing even had the power to launch nobodies into the best-selling list.

Polly saw pretty quickly that she didn't have it in her to be on every single social media site, so in addition to the FB page she's had since college, Polly added in blogging and Twitter. She also happened to read the brilliant, charming, selfless, humble and really darn good-looking Kristen Lamb's blog about building fan pages. Polly has a lovely page hidden, and every week she adds more pictures and blogs and links. The day she lands an agent she will unveil and invite all those FB friends she has been making over the past year to "like" her page…a page that looks seriously nifty by the way.

Since Polly blogs three times a week, every week, people have had time to get to know her and like her voice. They also take her seriously as a writer, because she acts like a professional writer. Polly's blog over the course of the year she has been posting has grown to where she has hits in the thousands. Last month her blog hits were 15,000 and climbing.

Polly was careful to make sure she was also learning about craft. In fact she networked with other bloggers who were blogging on craft, and she used their insight to write a truly excellent manuscript. Ah, but Polly knows that she has solid writing to offer...and also a blog following in the thousands. She also has had time to befriend other bloggers with followings even larger than hers...and since they like her, they have agreed to help her promote once her book is released.

An agent can Google Polly Prepared and see her name commands most of the first page. Additionally, they can pop by her site and see Polly has a regular following, because she has scads of interaction in her comments. There is a genuine dialogue with READERS! Agents dig that. They know it makes their job selling Polly's manuscript to an editor WAY easier.

Now this agent sees a writer who can write, and whose marketing reach extends....exponentially.

Who looks like the best bet?

Feel free to ignore Ned. Most everyone else does.

Creative Caroline might get an agent. She might even be successful, but she doesn't look like a good bet. Why? No one knows her. She didn't lay the groundwork for her fan base, and she is starting from Ground Zero. She will be half-crazy trying to build a platform and market so the first book doesn't fail, and this takes time away from writing her future books. That, and to be honest, there are too many other writers just as talented who come with a ready-made platform.

It's sort of like thirty years ago, if you had a four-year degree, you could write your ticket to success. Now? That four-year degree might keep you from serving fries for a living...or not.

I know you are wise people...you are reading this book. Seriously. You are professional writers. You have to own it, name it and claim it. If your family gives you a hard time, send them a copy of this book. And if they still give you a hard time, threaten to make them a character in your novel.

Writing is a tough gig, and it is tough to earn respect. But we fare better when we know what we are in for from the get-go. What exactly does our job entail? As technology takes over, I can tell you it involves way more than just the book. The cool thing is that we don't have to do this alone! We have a team to help. Blogging can make all the difference in our success.

Blogging—The 21st Century Writer's Quilting Bee

We just discussed the changing responsibilities of the modern author and how blogging is just part of the new job description. This happens. Times change and those who wish to be successful must grow and evolve or go extinct. The days of yore when writers could live quiet solitary lives is over.

We are part of a new age, the Information Age, and consumers expect interaction with their favorite writers. If we do not interact, readers will gravitate to those who do. We must serve the reader, which in a way means we are—gasp—part of the service industry. If we can visualize ourselves as part of a service industry, then we will see profound changes in how we approach blogging. I am going to give you a way to dramatically increase hits to your blog, while simultaneously growing your regular readership.

We have already discussed blog topics. If you are trying to build a platform as a fiction author, is it okay to blog solely about writing? Sure. Is it the wisest use of your time? Well, unless you are like me and selling mainly to writers, maybe not. (We will talk more about this later.)

My mother buys more novels than she will ever read, and she really doesn't care about writer's block, agents, conferences, or even the future of publishing beyond how it will affect me. To reiterate. Profile your reader. If you write sci-fi, what do sci-fi readers like to read and discuss in their spare time? UFOs, Nasca lines, conspiracies, Big Foot, Mystery Quest, etc. We have talked about all of this before, so nothing earth-shaking here. Ideally you will profile the reader and blog on topics interesting to them.

Now that you have an idea of potentially interesting topics, I recommend a new step that will help build you as an authority and is guaranteed to make your readers love you.

Find ways to use hyperlinks.

Hyper-what?

We'll get to that in a minute. First, permit me to expound. As bloggers, we tend to default to thinking like five-year-olds. Blog love becomes quantitative. Sort of like when Mom hugged on baby brother too much, we started plotting how to mail the little bugger to Kathmandu. We didn't understand that there was plenty of love to go around, that Mom wouldn't "use up" her limited store of hugs and kisses. Same with blogging. It is easy to get so focused on our own blog and our own stats that we forget the bigger picture....service.

The servant's heart is the single guiding principle in all my teachings. Service above self. What this means it that:

1. We must be vigilant about content. Content is to serve our reader, not our ego.
2. We must serve the reader by going the extra mile and providing an easy way to navigate the Internet.

The first step makes sense, but the second? There are all kinds of reasons that we might not get daring on the Internet. We are lazy. We are an instant gratification society. Hey, I'll admit it. I am the person who taps my toe as I wait impatiently the three minutes for my microwave popcorn. We are also overwhelmed. We are thirsting for knowledge while drowning in a sea of information. There are so many choices we are often on system overload. We are also fearful. Hackers, spyware, viruses, etc. are all very real threats, so we look to people who can help us navigate the treacherous Internet terrain in ways that are enjoyable and devoid of hazards.

As writers (bloggers), if we can appreciate this reality, we can take our level of service to a totally new level by providing an additional service—the hyperlink. Your readers will thank you.

If you read my blogs, you will see that every time I mention a book, I make sure to include a hyperlink to Amazon so that anyone reading could simply click and buy. That is a service. I try to always make it a point to include hyperlinks to any good blogs, or articles that might have inspired my topic that day.

This is one of the reasons Twitter is so helpful. When others "tweet" noteworthy links, I check them out. If I love the content and want to share, I make a note of the URL then compile them for a weekly mash-up (list of outstanding blogs and articles).

All of this is a service to my reader. I make it easy to purchase books, look at articles or read blogs. I act as an information delivery gal and as a filter, sifting through all the crap so you don't have to. Not only does this help you guys, my readers, but it also helps those who have been kind enough to provide us with something that would enrich our lives, our writing, or our free time. These hyperlinks bind us.

I like to think of hyperlinks like the stitches connecting quilt squares together. One square (my blog) might be intricate and unique, but alone it is limited in purpose. What can we do with one quilt square? Pot holder? Tea cozy? But, the real magic happens when we bind multiple squares (blogs, articles, etc.) together. Not only do we help ourselves and our readers, but we help others out there who are also trying to build platforms, sell books, etc.

Social media, in its finest form, should not be a solo effort, but more like a barn-raising—everyone coming together for a common goal. Or, in keeping with today's analogy, we are like a quilting bee, all sitting and socializing and sharing while working to create a common network of squares.

I chose the title *We Are Not Alone* for a very good reason. This is not traditional marketing, it is social marketing. Social, by definition, implies more than one. I challenge you to be an edifier and to focus on serving the reader beyond your own topic/book. People will appreciate your help and will often reward it with loyalty and patronage, not because you beat them over the head with a catchy marketing gimmick or free e-book sample, but because you earned that loyalty by providing a genuine service. Those people you take time to edify often will see that you included a hyperlink. This is not only a great way to earn their support, but it is also a great way to add members of their network to yours. Share and share alike, right?

How do you include a hyperlink? The simplest way is to just type or paste in the URL. The problem with that is two-fold. First, it doesn't look as pretty and can interrupt the flow of your writing. Secondly, it will likely navigate your reader away from your page—bad juju.

Thus, what I advise doing is that you insert the link into the text. When you are posting your blog, highlight the word you wish to turn color. This will serve as your link. After you highlight, on your dashboard, you should see an icon that looks like a chain link. Click that. A window will appear that will cue you to paste in the URL (you will see an http:). Paste the URL. Then, there should also be a Select Target box that will allow you to select whether you want the link to open in the same window or a new window. Choose a new window. This will embed a nice little hyperlink that now looks pretty and leaves the flow of your brilliance uninterrupted.

Summary:

1. Blog for the reader
2. Make shopping easy. If you mention your book, a friend's book or any kind of book, make it easy for your readers to click and purchase.
3. Include links to noteworthy blogs and articles. If you refer to one of your earlier blogs, include a hyperlink to make it easy for your readers to read that blog, too.
4. Include a mash-up
5. When you include a hyperlink, make sure you select the option that opens a new window. Keep people on your page as long as you can. We want this to be an enjoyable informative shopping experience. The less work you create for your readers, the more grateful they will be.

Now that we are recalibrated to start thinking like we are part of a service industry, let's explore how we should view our social media experience as an investment.

What Warren Buffet Can Teach Us about Social Media

I hold a firm belief that one could almost never go wrong using simplicity and common sense. Whether it is writing, marketing or life, I believe mentors can make all the difference. Want to see what success looks like? Study it. This past week I happened to watch a biographical documentary about Warren Buffett. Okay, I taped it on my DVR and watched it, then watched again and again and again. Buffett's approach to the world of finance reaffirmed my own beliefs when it came to my own unique approach to social media. Buffett's methods are simple and based on common sense. Most importantly, Buffett's system is for the long haul. As I watched this documentary, it struck me that many of his financial rules were highly useful for those of us building a social media platform.

Buffett Rule #1
Invest. Don't Speculate.
Great advice for social media.

WANA translation? Invest for your career. Don't be a social media day trader.

Social media isn't a fad. It is a fundamental shift in the way humans communicate. If you added together the membership of the top social media platforms, you would have the third largest country in the world, bested only by China and India.

Invest in social media for the long-term, especially as writers trying to build a platform. One of my students recently attended a conference and spoke to Kristin Nelson of the Nelson Agency. Nelson said her agency preferred new authors who had a social media platform. The other (unspoken) half of that sentence is, "…a platform that can translate into book sales."

What this means is that writers now have even more responsibility. We carry the largest share of the burden for our own marketing, especially in the beginning of our careers when nobody knows or even cares who we are. This can be terrifying, but take heart. If you want a career as an author, then it stands to reason that you would logically build a platform that can grow as you grow, one that has deep roots and can withstand the test of time regardless what social media site happens to be hot.

Buffett believes in investing for the long-term. Ignore the day to day whims and fancy of the market and look at the long-term prospects of an investment. I concur.

Blogging is a great example of a long-term investment. Do we wait until the retirement party to decide to invest in stocks and bonds? Uh, no. But there are many writers who plan to wait until they query, land an agent, or publish their first book to blog.

Blogging is a long-term investment. The prudent writer invests regularly, invests often, and invests her best. My blog is proof that this approach can reap tremendous dividends.

I began blogging regularly over a year and a half ago. I remember the days I got excited because over 30 people had read my blog. The day my hits shot over 300, I nearly passed out. Success was great, but it was super easy to get too worried about day to day slumps. Yet, I refused to let numbers get to me. I just kept going and told myself this was a long-term commitment.

After a year, the numbers leveled off as the readership became steadier. So I began investing more. Three blogs a week. The numbers steadily grew and grew. Nothing to jump around about, but impressive, steady growth. Then, one innocuous Monday, I woke up to normal hits. I went for a walk, and returned to over a 1000% growth in less than two hours. At first, I thought someone had hacked my computer. It looked like my blog had flat-lined and then had a heart-attack as you can see from the image.

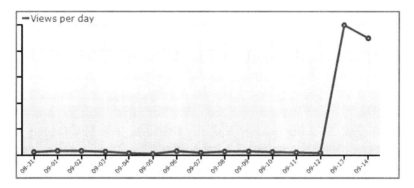

Then I realized the truth. My blog had finally been recognized by WordPress on their Daily Pressed. I was deemed the best blogger out of 370,745 bloggers. Talk about humbling! Of course, later that week, once I was no longer Golden Child of the Day, and the numbers weren't the same as that moment in the sun, but they were astoundingly better. WordPress exposed me to a whole new readership and my subscriptions skyrocketed. Better yet, I knew that if I did it once, I could do it again...then, maybe again (I actually hit the Freshly Pressed again four months later). This is the ROI of consistent investing. You can do the same thing if you are willing to look to the long-term.

When we think of blogging as a chore, it is easy to begin a blog and go hot and heavy for a month, burn out and then write once every couple of months when we feel "inspired." Hey, I've been there. Yet, when we look at blogging as a long-term investment in our future, then our attitude changes making it is easier to feel encouraged.

Want to know the best way to gain readership? Consistently post quality material that people value.

Buffett Rule #2
You don't have to diversify.
WANA translation? Ditto.

Warren Buffett feels that diversification is not necessarily the best approach. Can a person intimately know 50 stocks?

In my book *We Are Not Alone*, I teach how to have a presence on the 2 major platforms (FB and Twitter) plus a blog. There are all kinds of other valuable social media sites, but, like Buffett, I feel, "How well can a person know how to use and be vested in 10 social media sites?" There are gadget people, and I certainly envy them. They not only know every in and out of Facebook and Twitter, but they can tell you every detail about Squidoo, Technorati, Digg, Goodreads, and on and on. Go to their web site and there are so many badges in the sidebar it looks like the sash of an Eagle Scout. Yet, my concern for us mere mortals is…how well can one person know all of these sites?

Most of us struggle to balance family, a day job and our second job…writing. Now we understand that we must market and build a platform. So, let's say that is a third part-time job. How many of you have time to become a social media specialist, too? I say if you love social media and are good at it, go for it! But for most of us, less is more.

There is no need to feel bad if you aren't a member of every social media site out there. Pick good investments and go deep. Buffett's firm dominated Coca Cola because it was a solid company that likely would be around for a while. Facebook is a good investment. Some of the smaller newer sites? They might take over, but then we run the risk of becoming social media day-traders—shifting our investment from site to site hoping for a big pay-off.

Buffett teaches us that frills aren't a requirement for success. He is the richest man in the world, and yet he has never used a computer and has no calculator or stock ticker in his office. There are people on Wall Street who watch and wait and buy and sell and make and lose millions in a minute. Likewise, I am sure there are all kinds of methods guaranteed to gain one a bazillion followers right away.

WANA is not that method. It is absolutely frill-less.

Buffett Rule #3

Money isn't the only thing that motivates people. Never underestimate the power of praise.

WANA Translation? Free e-books are not as valuable as your praise and your service.

Buffett's approach to people is a huge part of why he is the richest man in the world. Buffett uses first names, is genuinely interested in others, and appreciates that people need to feel valued. He understands that other people are a huge part of his success, so he always treats them with kindness and goes out of his way to make them feel special. Buffett has been known to buy businesses for far less than others offered simply because the sellers liked him.

Social media is, above all else, social. All of my methods are grounded on the same Carnegie principles that made Buffett a billionaire. Serve others. Never have a hidden agenda. Want to get what you want? Help enough other people get what they want. Be genuinely interested in people, and do all you can to serve them.

Building a social media platform doesn't need to be terrifying or tough. Success has three simple ingredients. **Learn to be investors. Understand that sometimes less is more. Serve others.** Sometimes it is going to be hard, especially when we aren't an overnight success. We need to focus on what we can control, and learn to let go of the rest.

Let go? Yes. It is possible. We just have to maintain the correct attitude, as this next chapter explains.

The Attitude of a Farmer—Learning to Do Our Part

For years, I had a problem. Shocking, right? Like most problems, if not dutifully guarded, it still can rear its ugly head and make a raging mess out of my heart, my attitude and my life. What is this problem?

The need to control.

In the not-so-distant-past, my need for control often drove me to worry…a lot. To counter this worry, I planned for everything and felt I had to know every tiny detail and reason everything out ahead of time so I could limit any surprises. At first glance, that might not seem like such a bad habit, but, anything taken to extremes is always bad.

The thing is I was trying to control every little detail and all the players so I could somehow fix the outcome, and the end result? I was a mess. Frequently, the people around me were a mess as well.

Eventually, it became clear that I had to learn to discern between things I could control and things I could not, and then focus on meeting my responsibilities. See, before it was bad enough that I had to meddle, manipulate and plan, but then I made it even worse because I was expending my energies focusing on things I couldn't control while shirking duties I could control.

An example:

Will e-books take over and drive traditional publishing out of business? Will it be business as usual and e-books won't make a difference? Will small publishers reclaim lost territory?

Hold on: *consulting Magic 8 Ball.*

Sorry, Magic 8 Ball says *Reply hazy. Please try again.*

This is exactly the sort of discussion that I would have jumped all over and worried about. But through grace and a lot of tenderizing, I am a bit smarter. I learned to look to the farmer.

The farmer? Yep.

The Apostle Paul compares the life of every human to three

figures—the athlete, the soldier and the farmer. Something stuck with me about the farmer, and I didn't really know why. I mean athletes and soldiers are way more glamorous and more my style. Yet, the farmer kept popping up in the corners of my mind and convicting me of some really destructive behaviors, especially when it came to my writing journey. Successful farmers, like successful writers, have similar demands, routines and character traits.

A farmer's life is characterized the following ways:

Unrelenting Toil—Farmers expect work and lots of it. They know that every crop has cycles that cannot be disrupted. The land must be cleared and plowed then seeds planted. Then as the seedlings grow, the farmer is not shocked to see more work in store. He accepts that he must water and fertilize and protect the growing crops. Once the crop has reached a certain stage, it's finally time for harvest. Repeat.

Farmers work every day, not when they feel like it.

To be successful writers, we must also expect work and lots of it. We must understand that every piece of work has a certain cycle, and that if we skip stages there will be consequences that will be seen in our "crop." We are also smart to accept that, when we start our blog, we are planting a future fan base. It is defeating to expect a harvest three weeks after planting. To reap great returns, we must get in good habits—farmer habits—that compel us to work even when we might not be "in the mood." We have to learn to trust that one day our work will bear fruit.

The same thing can be said of our books. Whether books all go digital or stay in paper doesn't really matter. Our focus must be on the story. Our "crop" remains unchanged. Regardless of whether books are paper or digital, written by hand or printed by lasers, it will all boil down to, "Did we write a great book that people will want to read?" To write this great book, there are steps to take, methods tested and proven to produce great writing—research, reading, planning, proofing, editing, etc. Even after we have "harvested" there is more work in store. We must take our product to market. This means blogging, social media, speaking, signings, etc. This is why it is so critical to be planting our blogging crop at the same time. When it comes time to bring our work to market, all those great habits will pay off.

Protracted Hours—Farmers are up before non-farmers and work longer hours than non-farmers if they hope to have a great harvest.

To be a successful writer, we must accept that long and wonky hours come with the career choice. Also, in this new paradigm of publishing, we are wise to appreciate that writers who blog and build social platforms enjoy distinct advantages. This means even more work. Many of us have a family and a day job and we have to be willing to get up early, stay up late, or work on weekends. Do we have to put in these wonky hours? No, there are no Writer Police who will drag us away if we choose to invest less than 100%. . But what kind of harvest can we expect if we treat our "farming" like a hobby and only do it when we're in the mood? Do farmers wait until they feel "inspired" to plow fields?

Periodic Disappointment—Farmers expect setbacks. There are storms and pests and molds that can ruin months of labor. Farmers plan for the worst and hope for the best, but they always return to the land.

As writers, we must learn to expect set-backs and have a good attitude despite our circumstances. Above all, we must consistently do our part...and return to the writing. This is one of the reasons blogging can be such a benefit. Encouraging comments on a blog often serve to keep us positive. The networks we build are more than just compiling a list of people to buy our books. We are creating the team that will be there when we fall, and their support is priceless especially when we are facing a particularly rough patch.

Trust & Patience—Farmers are a tremendous example in trust and patience. Farmers, despite technological advances, still do what farmers did a thousand years ago but on a larger scale with larger harvest. They trust the methods of the past but don't ignore the benefit of innovation. Farmers of today worry about weather, pestilence and fluctuating market demand just like farmers did a thousand years ago, but they trust their hard work and planning to bear a harvest.

One of my favorite quotes is from Joyce Meyer. She said, "Patience isn't the ability to wait; it is your attitude while you are doing the waiting."

I wanted to be a best-selling author like Dan Brown overnight. Writing, for me, has been an amazing teacher of patience, a character trait that, frankly, I still wonder if I even possess.

Writers today do the same thing writers did hundreds of years ago. We have to capture an audience's attention and then keep it for the duration of our tale. We use characters, setting, narrative, dialogue, symbolism, etc. Like a farmer, the basics are still pretty much unchanged. Farmer: dirt, seeds, water and favorable weather. Writers: characters, plot, pacing, and favor from the audience. Even when it comes to blogging and social media, we are essentially building relationships. Not much has changed over time. Humans still want the same things. We desire community and purpose. We desire to be heard and engage in positive, meaningful ways. This is why gadgets and gizmos will only get us so far. Technology changes faster than anyone can keep up, but people are timeless.

Just like farmers have to grow crops comprised of tasty things people will want to eat (and part with their money to buy). We, too, as writers must create books people want to read (and part with their money to buy). To do this, we must trust time-proven methods while employing innovation and then have the patience to see everything through to publication. When on social media, we must offer content people want to read, and then share. We have to trust that consistency will pay off over time.

Farmers have a healthy respect for the things beyond their control (storms, drought, pestilence, disease, market prices, competition, etc.). As writers, we also need to possess a healthy respect for things beyond our control (agents, editors, publishing houses, contracts, distribution, rights, changes in the industry, changes in reader preferences). On social media, we must accept that we can only do so much to grow our blogs and our platform. We cannot "make" our content spread like wildfire across the globe, but we *can* form habits that make "going viral" far more probable.

There was a joke I heard about a delivery guy who stopped by a farmer's home. Farmer Joe was sitting in the rocking chair on the front porch.

Delivery Man: So, Joe. Did you plant corn this year?

Farmer Joe: Nope. Worried that corn mold going around would ruin the crop.

Delivery Man: Did you plant wheat?

Farmer Joe: Nah. Market rates for wheat have been terrible. Worried I wouldn't make a profit.

Delivery Man: Did you plant potatoes?

Farmer Joe: Oh, no. Was concerned the blight would get those.

Delivery Man: Well, what did you plant?

Farmer Joe: Planted my butt right here in this chair.

As writers we are blitzed daily with many things beyond our control. Are people reading less? Is the mid-list author disappearing? Will the bookstore be lost forever? Will traditional publishing collapse? But, while it is wise for us to be aware of our professional climate, there comes a time to say, "*Enough.*"

WE CAN control our attitude and that we are careful to do our part, every day in small ways. We have to trust that focusing on our responsibilities with a cheerful heart will one day bring great rewards. We must anticipate long and often weird hours. We must learn to trust time-proven methods and remain positive while waiting on success.

But add all of that together, and one day comes HARVEST!

I hope you are feeling really inspired by now. Sometimes the thought of having to market on social media on top of writing, researching, and family is overwhelming. It is easy to forget that, like farming, success really boils down to some pretty simple practices as this next segment explains.

Manners Count—3 Rules of Social Media Success

One of the biggest reasons I decided to write a book about social media is that it seemed that there was a lacking of common sense, and much of that is birthed from our own insecurity or lack of knowledge. When faced with something new or overwhelming, we often make life harder than it really needs to be. Hey, I've been guilty.

Social media is just that…socialization. I hear all kinds of bad advice when it comes to social media for authors, and much of that bad advice I believe stems from a lack of understanding about a writer's unique plight.

Until we are huge like Janet Evanovich or Dennis Lehane, we are people, not corporations. What this means is what works for corporations can actually hurt us as individual writers trying to build a platform. We need to act like people and socialize like people. If social media is, um, socialization, then doesn't it stand to reason that a lot of the same rules would apply?

How many of you love talking to someone who only talks about herself? She never gives back or asks about your day or wants to know about your opinion? Just on and on and on about her, her, her.

Have you ever had a stranger be really nice to you, maybe offer a compliment or even seem genuinely interested in you, but the second you let your guard down he tried to sell you something?

How many of you like door-to-door salesmen? Nothing makes your day like a knock at the door and some guy with a big smile and a freezer full of meat.

No one? No takers?

It seems we have become more isolated as society's technology has advanced. We talk to computers more than people. Checking out at a grocery store? Computer. Want your bank balance? Computer. Pay a bill? Computer. It also appears that this lack of face time has done something whacky to our human sensibilities. People talk less to each other and normal "rules of engagement" have gone by the wayside as we try to carve out new social rules for new forms of socialization.

But does it need to be that difficult? Today I am just going to point out some common sense manners when it comes to social media. Here are Three Rules to Social Media Success:

1. Be Low-Maintenance

How many of you just looooove high-maintenance people? No one? Then make sure you aren't being one on-line. I have been on Twitter or Facebook where authors have used pictures of their BOOK COVERS as icons, yet I had to solve a string of CAPTCHAs, know their real last name and their e-mail address to make them a friend. Are they on Twitter or in Witness Protection? These authors made it where only people with the secret handshake could be their friend. I guess those are the only people they want to buy their book, too.

True story. I actually tried to follow an author/speaker on Facebook who claimed that she teaches social media for writers. Awesome! I figured I might learn something from her. Problem was I had to answer a string of questions to be her friend. Seriously? Sorry. Not that motivated. Next.

Make it easy for people to befriend you. It is not that difficult to log in once a day and delete SPAM.

Making people on Twitter click on a website to verify they are human is being high-maintenance. Maybe it is a personal pet peeve, but I dislike anyone who makes me have to click on an outside link and go through a bunch of steps just to follow them. I will just move on to people who don't make me run a gauntlet to be their friend. My opinion is that, if you are that high-maintenance before I even know you, it does not bode well for our future.

How many of you like shopping at a store where they have security guards at the door, cameras everywhere so you can see yourself shopping, convex mirrors on every corner of every aisle, anti-theft tags on everything, and a burly guy to search your bags before you leave? Most of us really don't like being treated like thieves. Guess what? We don't like being treated like spammers and phishers either.

Again, it is not that difficult to unfollow someone on Twitter if they misbehave. One click. Two if you choose to report them to Twitter.

2.   Be Friendly

Treat Internet friends like friends. How many of you looooove SPAM and junk mail? How many of you feel really special when you get an auto-follow message? *Hey, thanks for following me. Check out my blog.* Auto-follow messages are junk mail. If you really appreciate someone following you, say it publicly. It serves reciprocity and it is genuine. It takes all of ten seconds to click on a Twitter bio or a Facebook page, scan, then write something personal. Don't have time for that? Fair enough. Most of us are not so insecure that if we don't get a personal message from every person we follow, we'll end up in therapy.

Yes, businesses send auto-follow messages, but businesses want to be perceived as personal. When actual people send automated messages, it has exactly the opposite effect. We become no better than a bot, which is counter-productive to building a platform.

3.   Be Genuine

Only send genuine & personal messages. Limit group messages and form letters. Social media is a direct reaction to the continual media bombardment that made us love our DVRs and spam filters. Facebook faced millions of ticked off users when they were busted for sharing personal information of Facebook users with companies for the purposes of soliciting. Why? Because many of us are on social media to escape being spammed all the time.

We are on social media because we long for community. We are not on social media to provide spammers a new way to slither into our personal lives. There are few things I find more frustrating than befriending a writer, only to be immediately blitzed with form letters and links so I can buy their book, read their blog, download free e-samples, etc. I have yet to buy a single book from any of these uncouth writers who vested nothing in our "relationship" before they wanted my money or time. Provide community and people will reward you.

I know there are times for authors to send group invitations, and that is fine for once in a while. Yet, it is my opinion this should be relegated to a fan page. We expect form letters and group invitations from Starbucks, not from a friend. We risk being perceived in a negative light if, straight out of the gate, we are blitzing people with marketing. Fan pages, unlike a regular Facebook page, are perceived to be our "corporate side" which is one reason they are beneficial for writers. They give us a way to take care of business without wrecking how people perceive us.

As a general rule, just remember that social media is social. Think of Facebook and Twitter like one big social event. A huge cocktail party.

Is it okay to do business at a social event? Sure! It's why I always keep at least a couple of books stashed in my car. Most of the time, in conversation, it comes up that I am an author and I have a book out. Being a prudent businesswoman, I make sure I can get them a book if they ask to buy one.

But don't you think I might offend more than a few people if I walked into the party, unfolded a card table, set out stacks of books and a credit card machine and then started pitching to everyone in the room?

In the end, this is just good old-fashioned common sense. Follow these Three Rules of Engagement and you will have a far better social media experience. If we are low-maintenance, friendly and genuine, we really won't have to work that hard. People will want to connect

Speaking of connecting, we are about to take on the blog! Yes, the blog! How do you write one? Where do you start? How can you get people wanting to read what you have to say? By now I hope I have converted you to at least consider blogging. Even if I haven't, these next lessons will still help you find ways to connect to your readers in authentic ways that create relationships. Best of all, these lessons are funny. Hey, laughing is good for the soul. We cannot take ourselves too seriously or this job will chew us up and spit us out. Time to have some fun.

Section Two—Eighteen Lessons to Blogging Awesomeness

Meet the Bright Idea Fairy, then Shoot Her—Lesson One

These blogging lessons are designed to take you from frightened newbie to veteran blogger in a shorter time then you ever imagined possible. Hey, I figure you would like to enjoy success while you are still young, right? You need to blog. Oh, I am such a nag! You also need to eat your vegetables, save for a rainy day, and always wear clean underwear, but back to our topic. Not only do you need to blog, but you need to blog effectively…in ways that will build your platform.

Stop whining. Don't think I can't hear you. This is for your own good, and you will thank me later. Everyone is telling writers to blog, but no one seems to be offering instruction on what to blog about. In this information vacuum, expect a visit from the Bright Idea Fairy. She visited me, too. So before we sally forth, I am going to just stop you before you do something…uh, dumb. It doesn't look dumb at first. I know. Been there. But I am here to explain why these "bright ideas" are time-wasters.

Bright Idea Fairy Unmasked

When we begin to ponder the idea of blogging, many of us will consider writing:

A blog about ourselves. No one cares about us unless we are a celebrity. Sorry. Just reality. Blogs should always be for the reader. If we are telling a personal story it must either have a larger message the reader can take away or be inspiring or funny. Tawna Fenske and Piper Bayard are two great examples. Both these ladies blog a lot of observational humor topics. So, if you are funny, use it! These two ladies are very entertaining. I don't care what their books are about, I know I will buy them because I love their blogs and they serve ME…by making me laugh.

Unless you happen to be a socialite, grew up in the circus, were raised by wolves, or have recently escaped from a sex cult smuggling

Chia pets stuffed with methamphetamine Pop Rocks, no one will really care about your daily life. On-line journals are self-serving. They are okay to have, but use them for what they are…journals. Not a substitute for a genuine blogging platform.

If you are a socialite-circus midget raised by wolves, you are excused.

A blog from our character's POV. This is a gimmick. If strangers don't even care about us and what we are doing, why would they care about imaginary people we made up? Seriously. Why would some random person who doesn't know us care about life observations from a fictitious character in a book that isn't finished or published? I was visited by the Bright Idea Fairy on this one, too.

There is no mistake I haven't made, no gimmicky idea that I haven't tried…and then found myself stuck in a tar baby. I am here to tell you to stay away from the tar baby with the cute button eyes and nose. Bad juju!

This isn't to say your characters and story aren't lovely or the next best-seller, but we have to look at WHY people love characters.

Why do we care so much about characters? Because we have been their partners in a journey against all odds. Take *Lord of the Rings*. We love Frodo and Samwise not because they are particularly interesting in and of themselves. We love them because we were there when the Ring of Power surfaced, and we followed their journey and setbacks and heartbreaks and triumph all the way to Mount Doom. We were afraid when they were afraid, broken when they were broken, and elated when they triumphed. Assuming Tolkien lived in a time of the Internet, having "Frodo" blog ahead of time about life in the Shire and his longing for adventure would just be...weird and kind of creepy. Definitely boring. It's like a stranger in the grocery store telling you her life story. Back away slowly. Don't make any sudden moves.

Stay away from gimmick. People are looking for authenticity. Give it to them and you will benefit greatly. No hiding behind your characters. If you are a new author, it is likely your first novel will never get published. It is likely your novel will be like my first novel and banned by the Geneva Convention as torture. So what is the point of putting all this effort into getting people attached to characters that may never be part of your published works?

All right, say you are an anomaly, and you do get that first novel

Kristen Lamb

published. An editor may love your story but hate your protagonist and insist she be rewritten....And then you are buggered because you have been blogging from her POV for the past year.

Or, say your editor LOVES that protagonist and the people following the blog from the character POV love your character. Now, every book from this point forward, you will have to start from scratch building a following. I am here to save you time.

How many books did Michael Crichton write before (God bless him) he passed away? We were attached to Crichton, not the countless characters over the span of his long writing career. I know no one will find you interesting in the beginning. Sorry. I am not interesting either. We will be one day, though. So until we become interesting, we must blog on other topics that are interesting.

A blog where we post sections of our novel. Yes, I did this too. Even if you are a good writer, posting any kind of fiction is just not good content. Why? Well, for a number of reasons. First, you need enough material to post regularly. With fiction it is going to be tough to generate enough content to make a regular blog.

Also, once you understand how search engines work (which we will talk about later) you will plainly see how fiction does not rate well on an Internet search. This means no one can find your blog. There is just better material out there to blog about that will help you grow a fan following for YOU.

So I hope I have convinced you that blogging can be fun and that is a great step toward being taken seriously. I know I probably shot some Bright Idea Fairies out there. OxyClean gets the blood out. Again, you will thank me later.

Don't Feed the Trolls—Lesson Two

Blogging is one endeavor that separates the real writers from the dabblers, hobbyists and dreamers. Why? Blogging is regular proof of what we are: writers. How is that? Um, we are writing. Duh. When you finish and publish your novel, then feel free to call yourself a novelist. Until that day, though (which likely will be a couple years in the future) you are a professional writer. What do professionals do?

Professional writers write. They don't make excuses. But I am here to give you fair warning. When you take on the task of writing a blog, just go ahead and expect that the Crappy Excuse Troll will rear his ugly little head—and it is up to you to kick him in the face. If you aren't hard-core enough to stomp him like a Florida water bug, then for the love of God, at least don't feed him. Then he shows up with his friends and starts adding crap to your grocery list.

• Saran Wrap
• Apples
• Peanut Butter
• Dishwashing Liquid
• 60 jars of Marshmallow Fluff and 10 pounds of chocolate
• Jumbo Bag of Rubber Bands and Jumper Cables..... WTH?

I don't know if you know this, but there are supernatural creatures whose sole purpose is to steal or sabotage your dreams. I've already introduced you to the Bright Idea Fairy. She is the creature who comes fluttering down with what seem like really cool ideas that are actually time-wasters in disguise. If you don't spot her and shoot her immediately, she can have you off on a primrose path of procrastination in six seconds flat. And, if you're not tied off to a safety line—which most of us don't run around with a bright orange nylon belt strapped to the plumbing—your blog or novel might not see you for months.

Like the Bright Idea Fairy, the Crappy Excuse Troll is on a mission to tempt you away from your desk with the promise of candy, a movie, or any shiny object that can gut-hook you like a trout. But, here is some good news. The Crappy Excuse Troll, while sneaky, is also fairly predictable. He is like that weird guy in the Wal Mart parking lot who manages to "run out of gas" every other day and yet people STILL give him money. Crappy Excuse Troll knows that his excuses suck, but suckers keep falling for them so he'll keep using them. Crappy Excuse Troll makes 12% commission off your shattered dreams, btw.

How do you spot Crappy Excuse Troll? Easy. He gives the same lies to every author. Whether you fall for them or not is up to you.

Oh, you just don't have time. With the kids and the house and the baby and husband and yodeling class, you are lucky to get sleep, you poor dear. Writing a novel has already been hard enough and NOW they expect you to blog too? Why you just can't FIND the time.

Crappy Excuse Troll wants you to believe that time is lying around like loose change in the couch cushions. It isn't. We have to grab hold of Time by the scruff of the neck and wrestle her down and let her know who is boss. In fact, just picture an episode of *The Dog Whisperer*, and Time is that pain in the ass Chihuahua who pees on your rugs and bites your kids. You have to be calm, assertive pack leaders and wrestle the pack of feral Chihuahua Minutes under your control. Time is not in control of us. We are in control of Time. Now pop Time on the snoot and tell it "Sit and stay," and mean it.

Now, when you do wrestle enough time to write, expect Crappy Excuse Troll to come from a different angle.

Oh, that is great that you are taking time to write, but 30 minutes is just not enough. If only you had all day to write.

Here is the deal, no matter how much time you dedicate to your writing and blogging, Crappy Excuse Troll will tell you that you aren't doing enough. Just expect it and then ignore it. You will be shocked how much you can accomplish if you will just dedicate even a half hour a day to your writing.

Crappy Excuse Troll, when he doesn't get his way, often will call in the Procrastination Pixies to give one last ditch to lure you away from your computer and crush your dreams. Procrastination Pixies, like the Bright Idea Fairy, are all sparkly and pink and sound like a good use of time.

Oh, I can't possibly write until the house is clean.
When I get an agent, then I will start blogging.
When I get a book deal, then I'll do social media.

Why does the Crappy Excuse Troll call in the Procrastination Pixies? Because they have the ability to take on human form. They can morph into our mother, husband, wife, children, neighbors or friends and lure us away with movies, errands, shoe sales and Happy Meals.

We can't let them win. Every time the Crappy Excuse Troll convinces us we can't possibly write for whatever good reason...a kitten dies. Kidding! The kittens are safe, but your dreams and goals will be eaten away one excuse at a time. We always have to be mindful that these supernatural creatures call out to all of us, like sirens from the rocks. We have to stuff cotton in our ears and refuse to give them audience or that is where our dream of being a full-time best-selling author will crash...on the rocks of *Gave it a Good Try*. By the way, those rocks are a giant graveyard for the aspiring writers. That's why I say forget aspiring. Aspiring is for pansies.

Why did I take the time to go through all of that? Because blogging for platform separates the writers who are trying and the writers who are doing. Be a doer. No one will take us to writer jail if we do not blog, but we must appreciate that other writers are blogging and are gaining a large following and that is the competition. This is like Rocky IV and the big freaking Russian is training in the lab with all that high-tech science stuff, and we know that we are going to be a red paste if we don't get in serious shape...fast. Grab a log and a harness. We're going snow-running.

It's the eyeeeeee...of the tiger. Okay, where was I? Right.

Before we go any further, I want to clarify. I don't care what you blog about. There is no right or wrong for blogging in general. But, when it comes to blogging for platform, with the goal of creating a large following, then there is right and wrong. I don't make the rules. I tell it how it is.

You can blog from the perspective of the fairy queen protagonist in your book. I will not stop you. Feel free to blog about your life and the tortured struggle to be taken seriously. You can even post your fiction. Again, I won't stop you. I will, however, tell you that it will be next to impossible to gain a large regular following in the thousands with those topics.

I am here to help you plan for the long-haul. If you desire to be a career author, then you need to put those roots in deep and plan on being around for a few decades. What I am teaching here is how to connect to a large audience to support you as an author. Are there super mega bloggers who use a moniker? Yes. However, their goal is not to build a platform to sell a book with *their given name on the cover*. Ours is.

Are you ready to be real writers? Then grab your gear and keep reading. We're gonna talk blogging. Many of you, when I shot your bright idea-fairies to show you how it's done, promptly had a panic attack and curled into the fetal position. *So much...blooood.* Okay, I'll stop *snicker.* Anyway, we keep posing the question, *"What do you blog about as a fiction author trying to build a platform?"*

There are two ways to go about this.

#1 You can blog on topic.

If you are writing a period piece, then blog about that time period—the politics, daily life, and the conflicts of the time. Many people who read period romances and mysteries LOVE history. I imagine you do, too, or you wouldn't spend time writing a novel set somewhere back in history. Duh. So if you love history, why is this so hard? Talk shop! Finally people who love to talk about the same crap you do. When you start talking about Elizabeth I or Bull Run, your followers will totally dig what you have to say...unlike your family whose eyes glaze over and begin drooling down their chins. Take advantage. Odds are you will even meet people geekier than you who can add to your flypaper of random seemingly useless facts. I can hear your leg thumping like a dog getting a belly scratch.

If you write thrillers? Again blog on topic. Blog about the CIA or FBI or Manchurian Candidates or current security threats. Talk movies. Write scientific thrillers? Blog on the latest trends in science. Read *Discover Magazine* or *Popular Science* and then tell us about what you learned in your own words. Blog on *Jurassic Park* or *The Fly*. Science or peek into the future? Write suspense? Blog on serial killers if that is what your book involves. Blog on forensics. Put all that research to good use. This will help connect you to readers who enjoy the same stuff. Trust me, the people picking up Tess Gerritsen's books are the same people who DVR *Criminal Minds* and *Las Vegas CSI*.

There are tremendous advantages to blogging on topic. First, you are less likely to run out of ideas and stall a month into writing your blog. Second, blogs on topic naturally lend themselves to discussion. People want to be involved and they gravitate to blogs that generate a dialogue. If we are just blogging about how tough it is being a writer, then we risk our blog devolving into weekly bitch session, not a thought-provoking dialogue. That is unproductive.

As I have said, the secret to blog success is simple:

Topic you are passionate about + Topic readers are passionate about = Hit Blog!

We are passionate about ourselves and our works. But we have to be careful blogging solely about ourselves. Do we like people who do nothing but talk about themselves? No. So why would that be a good plan for a blog? Common sense.

Serve the reader FIRST. Find the common passion.

#2 We can also blog by demographic.

I write books about social media for writers. What is my target demographic? Writers. Ergo, I blog on all things writing.

Writers do tend to be avid readers. Thus, they will be part of your demographic, too. So, if you want to blog on writing, go for it. Just make sure you are blogging about the craft of writing. Write blogs that serve those reading. You don't have to know everything. Heck, you can be brand spanking new. Even better. Get readers involved in a conversation. Tell people what you learned then ask for opinions, comments and feedback. People love to be helpful.

No one expects you to be an expert right away and that is fine, so long as you are deferring to experts. Now you have my permission to write about your struggles.

Today's blog is about POV. I have always found it hard to understand. Yesterday I read Bob Mayer's "The Novel Writer's Toolkit" and he explained it like this. Blah blah blah. Do you guys have trouble with POV? Why? Any advice?

Writers looooove offering advice. We are a very helpful group. And if you write good blogs, we will happily send our peeps your way. We love finding good blogs to help us improve our craft. If you love all things writing, then blog on writing. If you have 15,000 followers when your book comes out, they will buy the book because they like YOU and want to support YOU. That is the goal...for followers to like YOU. Not your characters, not your world, not even your novel. News flash.

Your novel will do that! Your blog is to get people to know and like YOU. **Your blog cannot do something only your novel can accomplish.** That is about as productive as trying to get your plumber to put in new kitchen cabinets for you.

I buy way more books than I ever read. I buy from people I know and LIKE because they have served me on their blog, and I feel it is my little way of giving back for all the hours they dedicated for FREE to help me. We need followers to like YOU if you plan on being around for a career...because I assume you have more than one book in you. Put your efforts behind YOU.

Whatever you choose to blog about, make sure it fits in the formula. You are passionate and readers are passionate as well. This formula creates a conversation between you and your readers. Conversations lead to friendships, and that is the goal. Serve your readers, and they will like you and will grow to be your biggest cheerleaders. Some of my greatest allies/promoters are peeps who follow my blog.

Okay, now the hard questions.

How often do I blog?

You need to blog (minimum) once a week. If you are blogging once a month or when the fancy strikes you, that's just wasted effort toward building a platform. Readers need to be able to count on you/your blog.

Me? I was a lazy sloth with zero self-discipline when I began blogging. I started with once a week then upped it to three times a week. In retrospect? Three times a week is WAY easier. You gain a following much faster, and it is easier to stay encouraged. I now blog four times a week and all on different topics, so I always have plenty to talk about.

I, personally, think blogging every day is too overwhelming for most writers and readers. I won't stop you, but my experience is three times a week is enough to keep you top of mind with readers, and not wear them out.

What if I started a blog about my characters, book, writing journey?

Keep doing it. Just pick a day for that stuff, then blog on topic the other two days. Originally I came up with *Free for All Friday* where I would talk about me and my book, but I just don't think I am all that interesting. I love being silly too much, and Fridays are normally my time to cut loose and poke fun at writers, writing, and the world in general. I am not saying you can't blog on that stuff, I am just saying it is a garnish and not the main dish. People want to chew on steak, not parsley.

Personally? I believe you could blog on Monday about writing, your topic (serial killers) Wednesday, then talk about you/your book on Friday, and that would be just dandy.

What if I can't find anything good to post?

Try harder. If you want to become a career author, then finding something interesting to say once a week should not be that big a chore. If it is, might want to reconsider career choice. We all get stuck. In that case? Read other blogs and get some inspiration. Heck, write a blog about our blog. We love it when people do that!

I do want to say that I advise you STRONGLY not to post sections of your novel. All it will take is some jerk posting something mean to crater your self-confidence. And DO NOT blog from the POV of your characters. That's gimmick. Steer clear.

Time to help you understand how readers will *find* your little jewels of brilliance.

Tearing up the SEO Killer Bunny Style—Lesson Three

2011 is the year of the Rabbit. That rabbit is DYNAMITE! Okay, so I had to find a way to make a rabbit seem badass, and that gave me an opportunity to use a gratuitous Monty Python reference. Making a rabbit seem hard core is not all that easy, you know. I want you guys fired up for 2011. 2010 was the Year of the Tiger. Easy. Then I looked up 2011. Year of the Rabbit? Great. *We dare not risk another frontal assault!...* ha ha ha ha ha. I'll stop. For those of you who have no clue what I am talking about, go to You Tube and type in "killer rabbit." You aren't a true writer until you quote Monty Python way more than is socially acceptable.

All right, time to discuss search engine optimization (SEO). I want you tearing up the search engines Killer Bunny-style. Don't panic. I am all about making this fun. And yes, technically I am making this Blogging Part III. Why? Because if you don't understand how search engines work, no one will FIND you. Okay, the site that sells Viagra and cheap Prada purses will find you. But we want readers to be able to locate all this lovely content that you guys are going to be posting in the future.

Most of you by now understand that you need to be blogging. That's great! But one of the big problems I notice among writers is there is a chronic failure to understand how search engines work and how to use them in their favor. What good is posting content if no one can find it, right?

What I am going to teach you here is going to help you rise even more above the masses of competition all clamoring for the public's attention and money. Unless you happen to already be a household name, your social media platform is more critical now than ever.

As a debut fiction author you will be competing against counterparts who have a solid social media presence and a blog following. Are you prepared? If not, the odds are not in your favor. According to the BEA, 93% of novels sell less than 1000 copies. A solid social media platform can make all the difference. Ask Amanda Hocking. She is a self-published author who sold 450,000 copies of her book in January 2011. Hocking landed a traditional deal worth roughly $2 million with St. Martin's Press. She credits the lion's share of her success to having a solid social media platform, which included a blog.

Earlier, we discussed using our names as our brand. Anything else will cripple a platform and leave an author stressed out and spread too thinly. Our goal is to get our names to do the heavy lifting (sales) so we have time to write.

Why is a name so important?

We are going to have a quick lesson on how search engines work, because there is no point in blogging regularly if you don't gain a large, committed following. By the end of this lesson, I am sure it will be much clearer why your name is so critical.

Think of search engines like a codependent personal genie bent on making you happy. Meet *Google the Codependent Genie*. Anything you desire is his will to supply. Google, your personal genie, will rush out and find whatever you require because he wants you to be happy and not have to wait.

The Internet is like one giant master closet full of everyone's "stuff." Now some people are like my grandmother and everything is neatly labeled, categorized and organized. Our personal genie can rush into the closet, look at the side of the "box" to the neatly typed label (tag), and know exactly what is inside. Yet, other folks on the Internet are more like my mother (okay, me), and they have all kinds of boxes that would have been labeled "Miscellaneous" if only we could have found the box with the Sharpie markers. So either there is no label or there is one giant vague label "My Crap" or "Writing."

So let's slip into the shoes of our poor little codependent genie, Google:

Oh, my little Google, you are powerful indeed. Here's my wish...

(You type) How do I write a prologue for a novel?

What your codependent search-engine genie SEES is...

How do I **write** a **prologue** for a **novel**?

Our little genie knows you get impatient and begin smacking buttons on your keyboard if you have to wait more than three seconds.

He also knows he has less than a second and a half before his mistress gets testy. And he also, also, also knows that if he takes too long or doesn't return with quality stuff, that his beloved mistress might decide to use another codependent genie (Bing, Ask, Yahoo), and leave him alone in cyberspace with no one to serve. If enough mistresses do this, he knows eventually he will fade away and die and be banished to the realm of AOL.

Our genie, Google, is very motivated.

So as Google the Codependent Genie whizzes into this giant storage closet known as the Internet, he knows that his fastest approach and the one more likely to return quality goods is that he needs to look at the sides of the boxes (think Internet files) for labels (tags). He glances at the labels and brings back the files that have been precisely labeled first.

These "labels" are known as tags. Tags are metadata, which means, "data about data."

When you add tags to your blogs, you make it easy for other people's codependent genies to go to your stuff first. The genie is not so different from us. He will look to the boxes with labels first. Only after he has located the "boxes" with labels will he then take the effort to look inside the box for what his mistress has requested.

How do I **write** a **prologue** for a **novel**?

Our genie will look for articles and blogs with those three words—**write, prologue, novel**—in the tags first, and only after that will our little friend sift through the body of the material for those words.

Tagged items will always be at the top of a search and on the first page. This will be important for later when we continue our lessons about blogging. Who among you go to the second page of a search unless you just absolutely have to? Tagging makes the difference between our stuff being first on the page versus being relegated to Internet Limbo on page 4.

Tags are also critical to defining you as an author (your brand), much like the boxes in our closets define us as people. If you went into my closet and noticed stacks of boxes labeled, guns, *Guns and Ammo* magazines, ammunition, survival manuals, camouflage, snares, rain gear, you would form an impression.

Similarly if you went in my closet and found crochet, quilting, cross-stitch patterns, thread, fabric, sewing, batting, needles, sewing machine parts, you would form a different impression.

What if you went in my closet and saw guns, romance novels, dragons, crochet, architecture, self-help, babies, cooking, Dr. Seuss, Martha Stewart, political science, 6-Pack Abs in Three Weeks, Judo, How to Train Your Dog? What impression would you form? Would it be positive?

Or would it be more like seeing a recipe that called for beef tips, chocolate, Marsala cooking wine, marshmallows, yams, jalapenos, corn, and jelly beans? Not too appealing, right?

Our blogs and our tags serve to define our brand. The content and tags associated with our name are important. What potential consumers, an agent and an editor see associated with our name is vital in how they mentally define us. Are they going to define us as *Quiche Lorraine* or *Dear God! Who Let the Kids Cook?*

As an example, here's my list of tags:

Kristen Lamb—Kristen Lamb, writer, author, speaker, teacher, social media, publishing, Facebook, Twitter, blog, blogs, blogging, We Are Not Alone—The Writer's Guide to Social Media, branding, marketing, platform, readers, indie, indie press, indie publishing, self-publishing, traditional publishing....

Notice all the tags were simple. These tags were all nouns that, if typed into a search bar, would serve to help someone else's little codependent genie find me FIRST. Generally with writers I see one of two errors. Either they don't use tags (or don't use enough tags) OR they use tags that are so obscure as to be ridiculous.

And yes, notice I put my name in the tags. Why? Because I want to become a brand name. I want that when people think/say, "social media for writers," Kristen Lamb comes up first.

Like, say "Tiger Woods" and...okay, bad example.

Say, "Warren Buffet" and you think "billionaire." Conversely, say, "billionaire" and one of the first names that comes to mind is "Warren Buffet." I want my name to do the same. Say, "Kristen Lamb" and people think "social media for writers." And— vice versa.

Also, what if someone meets me and all they remember is Kristen and a couple random details? But they liked me and wanted to buy my book? It could happen!

If they Google... *Kristen, writer, social media* then who will pop up? See, this stuff is pretty awesome.

Here's an exercise. Free write a list of all the words that you would like associated with your brand name. If someone forgot your name, but was describing **your work** to a clerk at Barnes & Noble, what words would she use? Write as many as you can think of and highlight your favorites.

You may also want to give a copy of this list to those close to you. Have them highlight their favorites or add any you failed to list. We don't see ourselves the same way others do and that will help you get perspective and eliminate emotional distancing. Some of us it took years to say, "I am a writer," aloud unless we had wine first. So how do others view you? It's important.

Also, go back through your blogs if you are already blogging. Do your tags make sense? Are they too vague? Too general? Too obscure? Are your blogs even tagged at all? If not, then tag them so people can find your content. We will talk more about tags here in a little bit. Have to spread out awesomeness so your brains don't cramp.

Some of this might not seem very pressing at the moment, but the savvy writer looks beyond the now and plans for her future career.

The Future is Now—Lesson Four

I am going to say something bold, but deep down I know I'm right. Blogging is the way of the future for anyone trying to sell a product, including books. Those who connect with their potential consumers and give a human voice and personality to their product will reap tremendous advantage. I know many of you believe me and understand that you need to blog, but I tend to be a person who needs to know why.

I want to put some things in perspective, and help you understand the why behind what we are doing. I am going to pan the camera back so you can see the big picture and where you, your book, and your agent (or future agent) fit in.

Agents and the Future

Want to be popular? Start gunning for sacred cows. Shove people out of their comfort zone and watch the fireworks. I blog every Wednesday on trending changes in our industry and give ways to keep up. But change is coming fast and some people are resisting. I can understand that and appreciate the desire to hang on to what is familiar. But my job isn't to make you comfortable, it is to prepare you for success.

Recently I had a somewhat heated discussion with a writer who felt I was out of line telling writers they need to blog to be competitive. Hey, can't make everyone happy, right? Anyway, this author adamantly defended that the quality of the book was all that mattered, and that an agent who wanted a writer to have a platform just might not be the right agent. Her agent didn't require that and so on and so forth.

Let's think about this critically for a second. I completely agree that the quality of the book (product) must come first. So let's just get that out of the way. Now let's talk agents and what on earth does that have to do with blogging and social media?

Kristen Lamb

I know many of you are dying to get representation. It is easy to put agents on a pedestal and forget what they do…. They work for us. It is their job to sell our work and command the highest price and the most extra goodies for that work. Conversely, it is our job to give our agent the most to work with.

What do you think will land a better deal? A very well-written book alone? Or a very well-written book combined with blog following in the thousands who know that author by name?

Your having a blog gives your agent an advantage when trying to broker a deal for your work.

Let's take this another step. We should be making sure that a prospective agent not only understands the current market, but looks to the future trends as well. Most of us want to be career authors, so we need to make sure we are signing with an agent who has vision. Back when I was looking for an agent, I almost queried this one agent until he rolled his eyes and sarcastically dismissed eBooks at an Agent Q&A. In my mind, this was a clear sign that he lacked vision. Not a good fit.

I wanted an agent who would push me to do all the things that would pave the way to a successful long-term future. I advise you look for the same. Hiring an agent who won't use e-mail and blows off social media is like going to a doctor who won't use modern fandangledy gizmos like MRIs or CAT scans. Could he do just as good a job? Possibly. However, would you feel safe putting your future in his hands?

Every teenager glued to his iPhone, every college student linked perpetually to FB, every grade school kid with a laptop is a glimpse at our future reader. A good book alone might be enough now, but my challenge is for you to plan for the long-term (and look for an agent who will do the same).

See, everyone is flocking to social media. Why? There are a lot of reasons, but I will only address two.

Practicality

Companies need to sell goods and services. Authors need to sell books. There is an old saying in sales, *Fish where the fish are*. News flash. The fish are all schooling on social media. Why?

The old marketing methods are failing. People use their DVRs and fast-forward through the commercials. We toss out mass mailings

112

as we walk in our front door. Radio? Try Pandora Internet radio. E-mail advertisements? We use spam filters or open junk mail accounts for when we are forced to give an e-mail address. We get people who know us to contact us via text messages or e-mail us on Facebook. Newspapers are fading into the history books, and many people no longer have a home telephone. The cell phone industry should bow down and kiss the feet of telemarketers. I believe it was their non-stop barrage of calls all hours of the day that got even the most technologically challenged to say, "Enough! Sprint, sign me up!"

If people are going to hear about your book, then it needs to be via social media.

Authenticity

In an age of plastic surgery, air-brushing and CGI, we are stewing in a sea of fake. There has been a recent trend toward that which is genuine or authentic. We are more sophisticated than ever before in human history, and many of us are no longer buying the carefully crafted marketing campaigns with airbrushed models and Photoshop trickery. We want to hear from people…REAL people. We pay way more attention to our Twitter pals or FB friends than any marketing trick.

If our Twitter peeps rave about a book, we know they likely read it, and we trust that opinion far more than a shiny placard in the front window of a book store.

The Age of the Writer

This is an amazing time to be a writer. This is the age we have all been waiting for. The time where we would RULE! I am going to give a little perspective. I have been a writer for years. I always found this scenario funny, yet it has happened time and time again (and still does).

So, what do you do?

I'm a writer.

No, I meant what's your job?

We do our job so well, most people don't notice us. Take heart and think about what we contribute. Ever been on the Internet? Like television shows? Thank a writer. Books, blogs, song lyrics, movies, video games, magazines? Thank a writer. Like knowing how to hook up your computer or work your microwave? Thank a writer. We are already an important if too often unnoticed component of advanced society, and I see a new and even more exciting role emerging for

113

writers...particularly bloggers.

Why Bloggers Will Rule

Lately, there have been posts that blogging is dying. That's crap. The blog might be evolving or changing form, but blogging is here to stay in one form or another. Well, at least until we blow ourselves up and there are no longer any humans who want to communicate and hang out with each other.

Okay, that's settled. Moving on.

Skilled bloggers, I believe, will have a distinct edge over their non-blogging or half-ass blogging competition. Agents with foresight are seeing that. This is why we are seeing more and more blog-to-book deals. Successful blogs come with a ready-made audience and committed following. This makes them a better investment for any publishing house.

Also, any agent worth her salt will tell you that only two things sell books: quality of the book (which is paramount) and word of mouth. Social media is becoming the new global village. Who are the villagers talking about? With some hard work and sacrifice, they could be talking about you. My blog has sold books and created fans in such places at the UK, Italy, Austria, Egypt, Thailand, Peru, Brazil and the Netherlands. Only on social media are we going to gain that kind of influence for the cost of a little time and effort.

Blogging is one of the most effective forms of social media for a writer. We are in the Information Age, and most people are on information overload. There are a gazillion things being thrown at us all at once. We have more choices than we know what to do with, more information than we could ever absorb in a thousand lifetimes. Now, with self-publishing and e-publishing, everyone can be published. The old gatekeepers are no longer present in the same ways, and there is more competition than ever before.

What do people tend to do when given too many options? They pull inward. They find favorites and stick to them like glue. We become like the kid with a bazillion toys who drags around that one ragged teddy bear with no eyes. Blogging is a powerful way to gain a loyal following and become a favorite.

How do you become a favorite? Actually, it is simpler than you think.

Kristen Lamb

The Counterintuitive Nature of Social Media; Sometimes Down is Up & Up is Down—Lesson Five

Forget reality as you know it. Right now, down is up and up is down. I am going to discuss the counterintuitive nature of social media. There are many habits traditional marketing has ingrained in us over the years that don't work well on social media. Yet, too many people still try to use old methods in a new business model, and that is like using parts for a 1990 Ford Tempo in a 2011 Audi. All you are going to end up with is a clunky disaster. A lot of smoke and grinding but little or no forward momentum.

First, we are going to discuss whether or not a blog can reach and influence fiction readers. A recent post by Best-Selling Author Jody Hedlund raised a lot of food for thought and highlighted, for me, how hard it is for us to wrap our minds around the real way social media influences. In her post, Jody posed the questions, "Do fiction readers read writer blogs?" and "Can a writing blog generate fiction sales?" Then, we are going to talk about some ways to increase traffic to your blog, and they may be very different from what you might imagine.

There are a lot of people who believe there is no way to market fiction. There are others, still, who feel that blogging is the realm of the non-fiction author. It is easy to see why people would feel this way. Social media is an odd duck and behaves very differently from traditional marketing we've been exposed to since childhood.

The top agents in New York will tell you that there are only two ways to market fiction (and even books in general). 1) We need to write a darn good book and 2) We need to generate word-of-mouth. That's it. That is all that can be done.

Traditional marketing doesn't work well for any kind of book. It never has. It is just the nature of the product. This isn't just my opinion,

115

it is a known industry fact (refer to mega-agent Donald Maass's *Fire in the Fiction*). Many of you might find this shocking. All those shiny bookmarks, flashy ads, book-signing tours and fancy book trailers actually have minimal effect on sales numbers. I was at a conference, and a big editor from one of the major houses told us they had a NF author with a book on personal finance. The publishing house paid big bucks to take out a full page ad in the Wall Street Journal to push this book…and nothing. This author's sales numbers didn't show so much as a tiny blip.

Even before social media, publishing houses would encourage authors to get in the mix--speak, teach, visit community organizations, do radio or television interviews (all still good ideas). An author had to connect with people and hope it would spark some good buzz. It is easy to see how this made it tough for the fiction authors. Most talk shows and speaker opportunities are going to naturally be inclined to favor non-fiction.

Back to good writing and word-of-mouth. I actually believe that the two principles work in tandem. Writing an excellent book is what gets people talking and generating buzz (word of mouth). In the past, fiction writers had no great way to influence readers or even future readers. Why? Because we were still dealing with traditional marketing. Most beginning writers don't have the money to go launch a flashy ad campaign to push their book and, even if they did, they could still expect a depressing ROI (return on investment).

But now everything has changed, and it is good news for writers of all kinds—traditionally pubbed, indie pubbed and especially self-pubbed. Social media gives an author the power to build a platform before she ever finishes the book. In fact, if done properly, a writer could have a following in the thousands before the book makes it off the press.

Social media works where traditional marketing fails. How? Social media is, by definition, criteria #2: word-of-mouth.

Social media isn't like traditional marketing. It is almost impossible to generate metrics capable of accurately measuring influence. Why? We aren't in control. As we've already mentioned, social networking is a way of approaching outsiders, getting them to trust and like us and our content, and then repackage our content to others. We are hoping that as we reach out to others, not only will we absorb their loyalty, but that their network will become OUR network. It's what I call The Law of the Playground.

I don't know you, but my friend likes you. If she likes you then I like you.

The other thing that we have to remember is that social media and blogging in particular is meeting criteria #2: generating word-of-mouth. We often will reach readers...just not directly. Our followers become the champions of our cause.

Jody Hedlund has one of THE best blogs on writing, and I highly recommend that you check it out. Can her blog directly reach readers who don't happen to be writers? Maybe. Maybe not, BUT she is being very successful at connecting with a lot of writers who like her, trust her and support her. Guess what? We have family, friends, coworkers, neighbors and random people we chat with in the bookstore. Whose book do you think we will recommend?

Psst—that's the whole word-of-mouth thing.

Also, many writers have large social network followings, and they tweet or post what books they are reading, liking, hating, or papering the bird cage with, etc. I know that when Jody's book *The Preacher's Bride* came out, half my family bought a copy simply because I like Jody and her blog (and liked her book). My family trusted me for a good recommendation. So, did Jody's blog influence my family? Yes, just not directly. Her blog hooked me, and I grew to like her and trust her for good content. Thus, eventually I felt confident and even excited to promote her book to others.

Did social media/blogging work for Jody? Yes. She hit the best-seller list on her debut novel. Is it possible to measure accurately what worked where? No. But, it still works, and that's all that matters. It is counterintuitive to trust that a loyal following of fellow writers is also reaching readers, but it is. Just keep plugging. Serve others, and they will love to serve you.

Okay, I hope you guys feel more confident that your blogging efforts WILL pay off eventually, even if you cannot observe it directly.

If you have been blogging once a week for a year and your hits aren't increasing as fast as you would like, post more often. It will improve your following dramatically. The larger the following, the greater the critical mass and better chance you have of hitting that tipping point that takes your numbers to a whole new level. When I

117

posted once a week, I had maybe 2700 hits a month on my blog. Within six months, my numbers shot up to 20,000+ hits a month and they are still climbing thanks to your support (and the methods I am teaching here). Some other ways to grow your following?

Pay It Forward--Edify/Promote Others at EVERY Opportunity

Include lots of trackbacks (links to other blogs/web pages) in your posts, and do a weekly mash-up. The best way to do well on social media is to edify others.

Comment on Other Blogs

I read a lot of blogs, and I go out of my way to write comments praising the work of others. Why? First, they earned my praise. But, I happen to dig getting comments from readers. I can't expect that which I am unwilling to give. Actively commenting on other blogs is a good way to gain the loyalty of other bloggers. Also, if we comment regularly, followers of that blog will likely become intrigued enough to click our name to check out our posts. This is a great way to expand our fan base.

Kristen's Rule of Social Media Success--Promote the hard work and effort of others more than you promote yourself.

This is counterintuitive to traditional marketing. Nike is not out there raving about how great Asics are. Guess what? In the land of blogs and books? We do better teaming up and understanding that love is best shared, and there is more than enough love to go around. Books are not so cost-prohibitive that people cannot afford more than one.

It is safe to assume that people will buy more than one book a year. In fiction, it doesn't hurt you to promote a fellow writer's book. Readers will read more than one novel a year. If they don't read more than one novel a year, it is still safe to assume they BUY more than one a year. Also, more often than not, that writer you promoted will return the favor. Though we should always promote others freely and should never expect reciprocation, people are usually pretty cool and will usually feel inclined to help us in turn.

In non-fiction? Again, readers will buy more than one book. If I were a betting woman, I would wager most of you own more than one diet book. I know around here, the diet books have their own shelf. Okay, shelves.

I am not worried about promoting another author of a social

media book. This other author may say something slightly different from me and it will click with a reader. I am here to serve others, and I have confidence in the quality of my book and the effectiveness of my methods. I also happen to believe that people are genuinely good and that it will all even out in the end.

My social media books don't cover certain topics that people might want to know about. I hope people buy my books, but if a reader wants to know about Digg or Squidoo or pod casts or building a web site, I forward them on to other social media people. But guess what? I have other social media people who recommend me as well. And, when we work as a team, we are something to behold. It is awesome.

Blogs are the same. Promote other bloggers, either by putting links to their blog in the body, or by doing a mash-up. Mash-ups are a fantastic way to spread influence. How? First, readers will come to trust you for good recommendations. Face it. We are drowning in a sea of crap and we love people who point us to good material. This will build your following because you have established yourself as a gatekeeper of valuable information.

Also, since you are sharing your network with other bloggers by forwarding your people to them, it is natural that they will appreciate you. This is a great way to gain loyalty of other bloggers and, as a result, expand your network exponentially.

I believe that writers confident enough to promote others are confident in their own content. Writers who rarely endorse other writers and who, instead, spam their social network with non-stop self-promotion, generally are much more insecure about their product. I personally, feel more optimistic about writers secure enough to endorse others, and I am MUCH more likely to purchase their books.

Promoting others in your blogs also has another benefit that might not be as obvious. It's one of those ways that blogs indirectly influence. We'll use me as an example.

You benefit from the work I put into my blog (hopefully). You reward my effort by subscribing or following. Many of you even go so far as to post the links on your FB, Twitter or blogs or even tell all your writing friends at critique (THANK YOU!). This not only benefits me, but it benefits every writer I have endorsed in my blogs. When you post my links, you not only expose your network to my blogs, but to all the writers I have taken time to praise. By endorsing others, I get to pay it forward. Other authors are able to be blessed by my good content, just as I was blessed by theirs.

Aside from providing great content that is reliably posted, actively promoting others is the best way to expand influence on social media. *Kristen! We hear you, but with so much to do, how can we keep it all straight?* Glad you asked.

Maintaining Your Blog and Your Sanity—Lesson Six

Okay, I know a lot of you are fired up about starting a new blog or even just buckling down and breathing new life into that old blog that's been invaded by dust bunnies and spam bots in your comments.
I so lick your blog. Is beste infermentation ever. My blog same. See you like. www.cheapviagra.com

If you are anything like me, you heard about blogging and took off like a shot. I opened an account, chose a ~~super~~cool background, posted a blog...then three weeks later ran out of something to say.

True story about how I ended up on WordPress.

I started on Blogger. I loaded my blogs then kept going to my link to look at my page, in awe that I had created something. Kind of like giving birth, but no drugs. I would pop over to ooh and aaah over my awesome turquoise...no, black background with red letters...no, flowers and babbling brook background with italics text. I would get misty-eyed at the sheer beauty and genius of my widgets (I had just learned what those were). *What are these?*

My blog is sooo pretty. She is the prettiest blog ever. I think I will call her Tiffany.

Even better was that, even though no one knew me, I already had 15 hits on my first day of blogging even though I hadn't yet told anyone. Proof I was brilliant and that soon the world would be dying to hear what I had to say. I was a blogging genius. I knew this every time I visited my page.

35 views! OMG!!!!

Hmmmmm. No one has left a comment.

Let me go check my page again.

36 views. What????? Wait a minute. Click.

37 views. WTH? Click.

38 views.

Are you kidding me???? Great, the 38 visitors were ME. Moron.

I changed over to WordPress because, at the time, the analytics kept me honest. Clicking on my own site didn't count.

Okay, yeah maybe I shouldn't have told you that story.

I be an expert :D.

The thing is I didn't go into blogging understanding what I was doing. I had a lot of trial and error and have had four years to throw noodles against the wall and see what sticks. Blogging can be the best experience ever, or it can make you hate your life, your computer, and your dog. Even if you already started your blog, these tips should help you as well.

Brainstorm

Before you start writing blogs, brainstorm. We have talked about blogging on topic or by demographic until we are blue. Sit down and pick a subject and see how many possible topics you can generate. Go for at least 100. Here is an example:

A writer of paranormal romance wants to start blogging.

Readers of these types of books generally like to hear about romance, the paranormal or even writing. Many writers are readers and vice versa. 78% of Americans say they are interested in writing a book, so blogging on writing is a good way to reach a lot of people. But let's pick *paranormal* because it is popular and makes a good point.

It is safe to say that an author who writes paranormal romance likes the paranormal. I think it is also safe to say that readers who eat up paranormal romance probably like *Mystery Quest, X-Files, Ghost Hunters*, etc. So a paranormal romance author could sit down and just start writing a list of topics that would interest people who dig spooks, spirits and stuff that goes bump in the night. Heck, as I mentioned earlier, blogging on topic is a great way to recycle the research information used in writing the novel.

Brainstorm possible topics ahead of time. You don't have to write about them right now, but that list will percolate in your subconscious. Your subconscious mind will become more in tune to the topics and will pick up on articles, shows, etc. that you can blog about. Sort of like, I never noticed red Honda Civics until I bought one.

Pick the Top 15

Pick your favorite 15 off that list, then take a day or three and write nothing but blogs. Load them into the queue. If your goal is to post 3X a week, you are already....

Crap. Need paper. Hold on. Carry the one. Multiply by pi. Why does it smell like something is burning?
You are already 5 weeks ahead! Now when you launch your blog (start telling people about it on FB, Twitter, etc.) your blog will look more professional and established. It is easier to be confident to send someone to our blog when we at least give the impression we've been at this a while and know what we're doing. I say fake it until you make it.

I try to always have a week of posts loaded in the queue. I pick a day and just write blogs. Then I am free to do the other writer stuff the rest of the week...drinking, prank calling my parole officer, bathing my sea monkeys, testing the viscosity of low-fat butter cream icing. You know, research!

Tag, Tag, then Tag Some More
Make sure you tag all of your blogs with your name.

The goal of blogging is to build YOU. I see too many writers who have killer blogs, but their names are nowhere in the tags. Go read Blogging Part 3. Google the Codependent Genie needs a hand in finding you.

After you tag with your name, go and add as many tags as you can think of that could be used in a search. In the blogosphere, the best way to find blogs, like anything, is word-of-mouth. But sometimes we just want to know about something, so we Google it. For instance, I might see:

How to Be a Better Author Blogger
Tags: blog, blogging, writers

Yeah, I see a lot of that. Three tags. Um, I want you to picture the Internet as one big carnival. Doing a search is like being at the ring-toss booth and our goal is the big pink unicorn (the loyal, subscribing readers).

Do you seriously want to belly up to the bar with three freaking rings?

Noooooo. Man up and bring in the real firepower. If that happened to be my blog? The tags would look like this:

Kristen Lamb, marketing, promotion, promoting, blog, blogger, blogging, write, writer, writing, fiction, author, We Are Not Alone, organization, time-management, success, platform, readers, publishing, Google, brainstorm....

Okay, you get the point. Be a Tagging FREAK! Own the Ring-Toss. Claim that Pink Unicorn! You are allowed more than three tags. They are free. No one is going to auto-debit from your savings account. Help your future fans find you. Now that you know how to be found, let's make sure your blog is ready for its "big reveal."

Kristen Lamb

Blog Fashion Faux Pas—Lesson Seven

Time to indulge in the blog version of *What Not to Wear*. We are going to pose the question, "What makes a great blog?" After a lot of noodle-throwing (to see what would stick) and tar baby wrestling, a book, and over 200 blog posts, I can tell you what makes a great blog. My blog has been very successful and grown to have a worldwide following because I have made all the stupid mistakes so you don't have to. You can bypass the learning curve and start your blogging off with a bang.

I wasn't always a good blogger and, in fact, when I look to some of my early blogs, I just kind of want to start whistling and walk away.

Don't make eye contact. Baby blogs not properly nurtured by humans go feral.

Content has been beaten to death, so let's address some superficial aspects of a blog that can make or break us from the beginning. Appearance matters. Yeah, we would all love to believe that we don't judge books by their cover, but most of us do...all the time. We aren't going to buy a house with the front door hanging off the hinges, a car the color of baby puke, or eat a gourmet dish that looks like something the cat coughed up. We don't go on a blind date and see some guy across the room and go, "Kafka! Kafka! That seems like someone I could have intellectually stimulating conversations with."

We are shallow! Blogs don't get a pass on human nature. We are going to judge by appearance first.

Time to do a fashion makeover on your blog. Does your blog have bad breath? Her dress tucked in her panty hose? A bat in the cave? Appearances matter when it comes to blogs. Let's check out some top blog fashion faux pas.

The Emo Blog

The Emo Blog is dark, angry, moody and most often

125

misunderstood. His black background mimics the color of his soul, and the red letters are like the self-inflicted slashes on his arms. Emo blog is just a bummer to hang out with.

The goth look is okay for teenagers who use their blog to catalogue teenage angst. If the purpose of your blog is to tell your friends about the time you dreamed you were Bella and Edward made you a vampire, then this background is fine. If you are over the age of 17, choose another background.

For the blogger trying to gain a following, tossing your readers' corneas into a Digital Iron Maiden is not a good way to get on her good side. Black backgrounds with red letters might look killer, but they are murder on the eyes. Any dark color with lighter lettering is generally bad juju.

There is a popular WordPress background that is turquoise with pale yellow lettering. Every time I click to a blog with that background, I move on. My eyes get strained enough without me volunteering for thicker glasses.

Yes, I will grant that these Emo/Goth/Dark backgrounds look super cool to us, but we already know what the words say (um...we wrote them). For a stranger, this will just make them hate us. It certainly won't encourage them to hang out and read our previous posts.

Blogs need light backgrounds, dark letters and, above all, must be easy to read. I feel for the horror writers, but there are some gray urban decay backgrounds that will be just as creepy, and the upside is that readers will be more likely to hang out on your site. Overall, when you choose a background, go ask the friend you can trust to tell you your butt is fat to look at your blog. Regardless of the background you choose, the point here is to consider the reader and the experience they will have visiting your blog.

The Poseur Blog

The Poseur Blog is the blog that just tries too hard to impress, and, in the end, just seems desperate and kind of sad. Italics, creative fonts, and too many flashy widgets are like two bottles of hair gel, a spray tan, an Ed Hardy shirt, and arms full of man bracelets. Sad, sad, sad.

Again, love your reader, love their eyes. If you must use a creative font, use it for the headers, but try to stay with standard fonts like New Times Roman or Calibri lest your blog be banished to the Jersey Shores.

Our content should be creative, not the presentation. When our blog has odd backgrounds with video, music and cursive font, this is the equivalent of sending a query letter written in pink on perfumed paper with stickers. Readers are judging us by what we write, not by the zillion flashy gizmos we learned how to insert into our page. Giving your readers a seizure from all the flashy stuff is bad. Again, less is more.

The Invisible Man Blog

The Invisible Man Blog has less to do with the content and more to do with the author. Where is your name? Is it easy to spot, or is finding your name like a frustrating game of "Where's Waldo?" Are you a blogger or in witness protection?

Our names need to be visible. If we are blogging and we are writers, then the blog needs to serve our careers. This is called "efficiency." Blogging and writing are not two separate activities. Our blog needs to build our brand, which is always our name. I have read some really excellent blogs, but had no clue who wrote the ███ thing.

You might be like me and you started the blog before you got a clue. No problem. Your name might not be in the URL, but it does need to be in the header. This is not the time to be shy. Write a blog you are proud to slap your name across...tastefully ;).

The Gypsy Blog

The Gypsy Blog has long flowing...everything. Long sentences, long paragraphs, long blogs. Looooooooong. The Gypsy Blog is so carefree that it forgot to care—at all. I know there is a lot of debate how long blogs should be. Personally, I don't care. If a blogger is keeping me engaged and entertained, word count is the last thing I am paying attention to.

The trick with length is to make the paragraphs smaller. Break a long blog into digestible bites. As long as you are writing in a way that engages the reader, likely she won't notice if you run long. Trust me, a 500 word blog in 9 font that is all one paragraph will get skipped before a 1200 word engaging blog with larger font and lots of breaks.

I hope that I've convinced you. Topics and presentation do matter. But, you might still be wondering what makes the difference between a good blog and a GREAT blog? How can you tweak your message to build rapport and resonate with your readership in ways that have them begging for more? Read on.

Connecting with the Readers—Lesson Eight

Time to discuss ways to make our blog connect with our readership. I read too many blogs that sound like the author is lecturing, ranting, or having a party all to herself. Those blogs do not connect with me, and I doubt I'm alone in this. I have to admit, in the beginning, I was a lousy blogger. Make no mistake, I was an excellent writer, but blogging is more than preaching...it's connecting. When I look at my early blogs, I see how my language, my topics and even my writing "voice" failed to connect with the reading audience.

Actually, the tactics I will show you here are so simple you are probably going to smack your forehead. So much of this is common sense, but as humans (particularly writer humans) we love to overcomplicate things. This is why I suck at True and False. Choose ONE? Can't I write an essay? Why am I sweating? Is my shirt on backwards?

Dichotomy is my enemy. Back to blogs.

When we decide to vest ourselves in social media, it is smart for us to pull back from the gidgets and gadgets and whats-its to look at WHY people are on social media. What do they want? Information and entertainment. No, what do they really want? Connection. Noooo, what do they really, really want? Relationship. We are people, and we need connection and community to stay sane. We crave attention and praise, and we like to feel as if we matter. People who intrinsically understand this principle will enjoy far more success in all realms of social media, whether it is a blog, a tweet or even a status update.

Feed the real need. Relationship.

How are relationships created? With dialogue. Have you ever met someone who was witty and charming and interesting...but they never shut up (*whistles and looks away guiltily*)? They go on and on dazzling you with stories and jokes, yet there is still something lacking.

On the other hand, have you ever met someone who asked about you? Your thoughts, your opinions, and your ideas? They patiently listened and even seemed interested? We LOVE these people, but they are so rare.

Why?

I believe it has to do with fear. We feel we don't have much to offer so we put on a good show, failing to understand that we don't have to jump out of planes or go on safari to be interesting. **All we have to do to be perceived as interesting is to genuinely be interested**.

If you go back and look at the early posts on my blog, it is easy to spot that I was very insecure. You can also see that I really wasn't engaging with readers. How? Very few comments, but we will talk on that more in a bit. Thus, though trial and error, I have found some ways that can make your blog feel more intimate and engaging.

Pay Attention to Your Pronouns

Throughout these blogging lessons I have emphasized over and over that we are serving the reader first. Our blog is a service. We must be careful how many times we use the pronouns "I" and "you."

If our blogs are full of sentences with "I, I, I, I, I," then we risk coming across as self-centered. We will be like that person at the party who only talks about herself. Can we use "I?" Yes, duh. We just need to do a quick sweep and make sure we don't have a personal pronoun infestation. If we go on and on with "I, I, I, I," it makes it hard for readers to feel as if they are part of a conversation and leaves them feeling like spectators. This isn't entirely bad, but blogs that grow the fastest create dialogue.

"You" is another pronoun that can get us in trouble. How? Subconsciously, it places the author and the audience on opposing sides of a dividing line. One is right and one is wrong. Too many "you, you, yous" and the reader likely will feel more like she's being lectured or chastised, and that doesn't make for a positive experience this reader will want to repeat.

Notice I go out of my way to use "we," "us," and "ours." Why do I do that? First of all, it is because I need to be mindful that I am not above my own advice. Also, because most of my blogs are instructional, using inclusive pronouns is the best way for me to calm your nerves, ease your fears, and help you begin to feel as if you are part of my team...which you guys are. It is my subtle way of joining forces with you. Choosing inclusive pronouns subconsciously impresses on you (my readers) that I am on your side, and that social media is our collective endeavor...because it is!

Additionally, and perhaps most importantly, I wasn't born knowing social media. Most self-help or instructional experts would be wise to admit openly that they weren't always perfect. It connects us as teachers to those who desire to learn from what we have to say. We can be professional and empathetic without losing the respect of others. In fact, when we come down to a human level, it helps our audience learn faster because it peels away that layer of fear. Our audience feels as if we understand them on a far more intimate level because we have battled the same dragons.

Ask Questions

As a social media "expert" it is really easy to slip into "Know-It-All Mode" super fast. I used to feel that asking questions at the end of a blog was dangerous for a NF author, but I believe that was from my own insecurity at the time. People who are truly secure do not mind a different perspective, and, in fact, should welcome it. I grow every day from the comments posted on my blogs. Many of my readers have life experiences and insight that offer a totally unique perspective I might not have thought about. When readers offer comments, insights and opinions, it challenges me and makes me grow. It offers fresh content that makes my teachings more dynamic. I don't always have to agree, but if I am confident in what I know, then a different opinion (offered respectfully) should be welcomed.

Dialogue is very important. Try to have questions at the end of all of your posts. Actively spark conversation. In fact, often I reserve information, because I like challenging you, my readers, to rise to the occasion and give your thoughts. If I cover every detail, then not only does that make my blog too long, but then no one has anything to add. What fun is that?

Look for the Common Emotional Ground

We can blog on all kinds of topics, but the ones that will resonate are the ones with a central theme. Common emotional ground builds instant rapport. For instance, I could tell some great tales of living in a refugee camp in Syria (which I did). The story would probably be interesting and allow me to impress people, but would it engage them?

What if I took it to another level and added a universal theme? Instead of trying to show off for my readers by focusing on life among the Bedouin and the refugees, I could, instead, talk about the profound loneliness of living so far away from home surrounded by people I couldn't communicate with effectively (my Arabic was less than stellar). Almost everyone can relate to being homesick or lonely or misunderstood. Now this exotic story (blog) is far more intimate, and opens a way for readers to offer their stories and, ultimately, connect.

Most of us feel a need to be heard and understood. We long for relationship and like people who care about what we have to say. As bloggers, if we will give others something more to take away than simple entertainment or information, we have the foundation for a hit blog.

Advertising—Selling Our Blog to the Readers—Lesson Nine

We must always be mindful how we are portraying our blogs to others. Let's think of it as advertisement. What are we really telling others about our blogs (us)?

Writing is an emotional business. In the creative fields, we pour our hearts and souls into our work, then thrust it out for display, and hope people like it, even though, deep down, we default to expecting a barrage of rotten vegetables to come hurdling through the screen.

So what do we do to protect ourselves? We emotionally distance, which is bad, bad, bad. We think our comments will get us *gratis*, but, instead, all they do is alert others to our faults. For instance, "Oh this is just something I threw together." This (we think) is a cushion in case other people don't like our content. Yet, all it does (in truth) is draw attention to mistakes that they might not have noticed had we not inserted the emotional bumper.

My goal is for you to use blogging to build a platform to support and grow a successful career. We need to think of our blogs as the storefront of our operation. Our blog is the hub where people interact with us and our writing. It is the place where potential supporters/readers form their opinions.

Our blogs influence opinions, positively or negatively. So what message are we sending to others?

Blogging Habits

If we blog when we feel like it, this is akin to opening the store when we need some cash or because we feel particularly inspired to work that day. I won't dwell in this too long because it has already been discussed in detail in earlier lessons. Suffice it to say that the better the blogs and the more consistent and dependable, the better opinion others will have of our blog and of us.

Blog Content

We've also discussed content. Focused content builds a brand. It helps form an opinion of who we are as a writer. Content is like the ingredients on the back of a label.

If I hid a certain product from you and merely read off the ingredients:

Organic Tomato Puree (Water, Organic Tomato Paste), Organic Diced Tomatoes in Juice, Organic Extra Virgin Olive Oil, Organic Onions, Organic Sugar, Sea Salt, Organic Oregano, Organic Garlic, Organic Basil, and Organic Black Pepper.

From this list of ingredients, would you feel pretty confident guessing what the product was?

Pasta sauce, right? And likely a high end pasta sauce since everything had "Organic" in front of it.

Our blog content tells others who we are as authors (product). We don't have to post chapters of our book for readers to get a taste of our writing voice, even if we are shifting over from NF (blog) to fiction.

Author Chuck Wendig is brash and viscerally descriptive, whether it is his awesome blog (which usually talks about writing) or his novels or short stories. When I read *Irregular Creatures*, I was not thoroughly shocked that Chuck wrote it. His razor-sharp wit, authentic voice and amazing use of imagery made his fiction just as enjoyable as his blog (his blog actually is what sold me to read his fiction in the first place).

If our blog is our storefront operation, then what can customers (readers) expect to be out for display? Important question to ask before launching any blog. If your blog is up and running, does it need more focus? Is it too broad? If you are blogging on broad topics, can you link them with a theme?

But, you guys are smart and know content is important. All of this brings me my most important point, the single largest way people judge us and our blogs.

We tell others how to judge our blog.

What are we saying about our blog? There is one word that I wish I could eradicate from the vocabulary of all bloggers. What word is this? *Ramblings*. I HATE that word, and when I was new and insecure, I used it too. And, yes, Chuck uses it, but it fits Chuck's image of a Genius Word Pirate with Tourette's (and his blogs are actually highly focused).

For the rest of us mere mortals, "ramblings" is a negative word. This is like opening a company that jars homemade sauces and naming the product, "Crap We Threw in a Jar." Hope you like it.

Words like ramblings and musings tell potential readers that there was little to no forethought put into our content (which might not even be true). No need to argue with me. This is all my opinion. Back to *ramblings* *makes sign of the cross.*

Let's just think about this for a second. Do we like being in conversations with people who ramble? No! We check our watch and hope a friend passes and rescues us. We search our mind frantically for a way to politely disengage from people who ramble. We hide our head in the freezer case when we see them in the grocery store and hope they pass before frostbite sets in.

Yet, I see too many writers tweet about, "Oh, posted some ramblings on my blog." Why do we think that will make people want to drop everything to come read our blog? We aren't offering anything of substance. Well, we might be, but we just told everyone that we put no planning or thought into our content. I see too many writers using these kinds of adjectives, and I have to say that there are generally only two reasons to use the words ramble, musing, random, or any variation thereof.

1). **We want to emotionally distance from rejection.** I started a blog years ago that was "Kristen's Random Musings." Gee, I wonder why people weren't lining up to read my blog. But it was such a huge step to put myself out there, and I was terrified of the digital cabbages I just knew would be lobbed at me any moment. The problem is that *the words we use to cushion us from failure are often responsible for the failure.* We are being self-defeating.

We are like the person who goes on a date and says, "I don't know why I have never been married. Most of my dates go great the first time, but then the guy never calls back." Um, the guy probably isn't calling back because he figures the dudes before him might have been on to something that he missed. He will be watching every move and paying attention to every mistake made during dinner. Why? Because we TOLD him to.

2) **We have no idea what our content is, but rather than commit to something (and risk failure), we cover our lack of**

preparation with adjectives that sound pretty—ramblings—but, in reality are very negative.

When we tweet about our blog or announce it on FB, we must always be mindful that we are putting our best foot forward. If our blogs aren't serving others, then this is harder to do. This is one of the reasons that using our blog for an on-line journal or putting up sections of fiction make it hard to advertise a blog. It's like trying to operate a business that has nothing for sale, nothing to offer a customer. That's a museum, not a storefront.

Blogs that gain large followings serve our readers; they aren't monuments to us. By the time our writing is worthy of a monument, we won't have time to blog, and our fan clubs can erect monuments to our awesomeness. Then it's less weird.

And, if you are insecure? My best advice is to "act as if." Often we are our harshest critics, and we think people are actively looking for when we screw up. Really, they aren't. At least not the majority of people. Just keep writing and keep focusing, and, as your following grows, your confidence will too. No sabotaging.

After these nine lessons, I hope you feel far more confident about your blogging future. But, alas, the blogs will not write themselves and we are back to talking about healthy habits that can make for a successful writing career.

Product Trumps Promotion—Lesson Ten

I freely admit that the fantastical world of blogging can offer authors tremendous advantages, but I want to make something crystal clear. I have always stated that I am a writer first, social media expert second. Why is that? Because the product is the most important. No social media platform can help us if our product is crap. No blog can help sell unfinished books. We must always keep perspective if we hope to be successful author-bloggers.

Blogging is probably THE best way to build a platform, but we must always be vigilant that it does not take over our main job, which is writing books. Blogging is instant gratification, whereas a novel or even a NF book might not give us warm fuzzies for months or even years. It is very easy to get so focused on the blogging, that the real writing never happens.

I love to watch Gordon Ramsay's *Kitchen Nightmares,* and have used his show as a parallel for the world of writing in numerous blogs. Every episode begins the same. A new restaurateur sits eagerly awaiting the great Chef Ramsay. Keep in mind that this restaurateur is only on the show in the first place because he sits on the verge of losing everything—business, house, car, kidneys, etc.

Most restaurant owners who participate have waited until the situation is so dire that Vinnie the Crowbar is only kept at bay because of the presence of Gordon's camera crew. Gordon is there to sample the food, and take a look around. Once he has enough information, Gordon then offers his professional opinion and a plan to turn things around (if that is even possible).

I've watched at least eight seasons of shows and almost every time, the problem is simple. The food sucks. No matter how pretty the décor or how clever the promotions, all that matters in the end is good food. Not rocket science. Yet, time after time, Chef Ramsay discovers the chefs are serving frozen, old and even rotten food.

The owners have no idea why the dining room is empty, no clue that it might have to do with the spoiled crab and rancid chicken they are serving the customers. In 50 or so episodes I cannot recall a single episode where the restaurant was serving quality food. The problem always came back to the core—the food.

Good news spreads fast, but bad news spreads faster. Same with our books. One of my favorite quotes is from PR expert Rusty Shelton. He says, "Social media helps bad books fail faster." One of the biggest reasons I blog about writing on Monday, is that the single best thing we can do for our image and to sell books is to write great stuff. That simple. No magic formula.

The best thing we can all do for our social media platform is to focus on the product—our writing—FIRST. Everything else is a supporting goal.

Back to blogging.

Blogging is a two-edged sword. To be fair, we need a little instant gratification. Instant gratification can be very important. It keeps us encouraged and makes us work harder. Face it. It could be years before we get any sense of fulfillment from our novel. It is hard to stay on track without a little boost, and blogging is definitely good for that. We get rewarded almost instantly for good behavior, and blogging offers the validation and the encouragement we need.

Be careful.

Blogging can be masking our fear. I love to blog. My followers are the highlight of my day and their comments are like manna from heaven. Yet, I have to make a deliberate effort to get back to the writing my followers can't see (yet). Since I don't get that instant validation on the other work, it is easy to become fearful of failure and use blogging as busy-work. I can be "productive" without being productive.

In *Kitchen Nightmares* it is very common for Gordon Ramsay to inspect the walk-in refrigerators and find something out of a horror movie—buckets of decaying meat and crates of vegetables that have rotted to ooze. In some cases, I find it amazing these establishments haven't killed their customers.

Yet, despite the hot zone in the fridge, the owner is ordering more and more and more food. Crates of fresh food are perched on top of the putrid slime that once was chicken. Why? Because the owner is so afraid and so overwhelmed that all he knows to do is order more food. He is throwing away thousands of dollars to "feel" productive, and is too overwhelmed and terrified to get to the heart of the problem.

Blogging, if we aren't careful, can be our way of throwing fresh food on top of rotten product. Writing is scary. Admitting we don't know everything or even facing that we might not be as talented as our family thinks we are can be terrifying. But, in the end, if we want to succeed at this writing thing, then the tough work must be done. We have to get rid of the rotten—the bad habits, the info dump, the POV problems—and that will take hard work.

Sometimes, it will even require professional help. Ramsay has had restaurants with kitchens and refrigerators so filthy that he had to call in professional cleaning crews to handle the bio-hazards correctly. The owner was so overwhelmed that he simply could not dig himself out.

Our first novel might be that bad. Hey, we're learning! I know my first novel (years ago) required professionals to properly dispose of the remains. My book just couldn't be saved, and there I was, putting a halt to my writing future by holding on to something rotten.

I would love everyone to blog. I love blogs. But I want to make it clear that it is easier to be a great blogger if our bad novel isn't clawing at the inside of our computer screen trying to escape and bite others. **Blogging can be a short-term high that can sabotage long-term success.** There are few things that will make you feel better about your career than watching your following grow on your blog. But the point of all of this social media stuff is to eventually sell our *books*. Otherwise, we are working for free and then we are right back where we started. We are hobbyists and not true professionals.

In the end, we must do both. We must write our books and we must build a platform to support the future sales of those books. This is a tough job. There are many, many reasons this career is not for everyone. We are much like the restaurant owner. We must focus on content that is fresh, new, inviting and tasty. But, until we are an established name, good food will only take us so far. We need to market as well. It will take years of producing a great product (books) **balanced with** great marketing to give us a reputation that needs no introduction.

Opportunity Come in Overalls—Lesson Eleven

Many writers panic when they are told they not only need to write, but to create a social media platform as well. Hey, I feel your pain. In fairness, we don't HAVE to do anything but write the book. But, we do need to ask ourselves if we are doing everything *in our power* to help our career . . . and be honest.

Thomas Edison said, "Opportunity is missed by most people because it is dressed in overalls and looks like work."

The paradigm is shifting in publishing and yes there is a lot of work put on our plate, but *with this extra work*, we will enjoy advantages no other writer in the history of publishing has ever enjoyed. We exercise much more control of our destiny than any writer EVER.

Product reigns supreme. I don't care how many millions you spend launching fish-flavored ice cream with caviar sprinkles, it's going to flop (no pun intended). We must focus on the product and that our book is something others want to consume.

But, not to be a smar . . . we always had control over that.

We always had control over writing a great book and yet 93% of novels sell less than 1000 copies (per BEA statistics). Why? Did 93% of writers write a crappy book? I doubt that. This hellish statistic, I feel, was due to that fact that until very recently fiction writers had little to no control over building a platform. They were throwing a damn good product into the night and hoping to hit something. Only a small percentage could expect to survive and thrive long-term.

For ages writers have griped and complained (justifiably) that they didn't get enough marketing support. Well, now we have a way to generate word-of-mouth and build a brand for FREE. We have to ability to spread word about us and our books to thousands and even tens of thousands of people . . . but it is too hard.

We won't have time left over to write, we whine.

Yes . . . yes we will. We just have to make key decisions and some sacrifices. But with a solid plan, hard work and time-management, it is doable.

Anything in life worth having takes hard work. Some people might believe that I am telling people to blog away their day and ignore the book. I don't know why anyone would think that since I blog every Monday to help writers with craft. But, hey, misunderstandings happen. When it comes to writing fiction, if I don't know something or it is beyond my realm of expertise, you can count on me to at least point you guys to books, speakers and workshops to fill in the gaps.

Good writing is essential, but social media is critical as well.

Writing and social media are like eating healthy and working out put together.

To let you in a little into my world.

I had a baby last year. I worked out every day I was pregnant until the very end, and I was eleven days past due. I spent forty-five minutes on the elliptical then went to the hospital to have my son. I had been so good.

Now you need to understand a little about Kristen. I was the WORST . . . the biggest lazy sloth on the planet. The only way you might see me run more than a mile would be if there was a psycho swinging an ax behind me. Even then, after a mile or two I would probably have let said ax murderer just end my suffering. I have always struggled with laziness.

I would start to the gym, go hot and heavy then get too sore, injured or bored. Then, I would give up and eight months later be back at it. When my husband and I found out a baby was on the way, I cleaned up my act. I ate perfectly and exercised every day. I didn't want to gain a bunch of weight that I wouldn't be able to get off. Let's say I was very motivated.

Eleven days after I had my son, I began working out, but I wasn't as good about watching my diet. Though I worked out all the time my weight dropped at a snail's pace . . . if the snail was a heavily sedated snail weighted with barbells.

I flipped the other direction. I started eating really healthy, but I started putting off working out. Again, my weight dropped at glacial speed. At the rate I was losing weight all my clothes would be long out of style before I could wear them again.

But, I had to ask myself the hard questions. Was I comfortable being fluffy for good? I could eat whatever I wanted and work out OR eat healthy and sit on my butt, but then I had to be happy being thirty pounds heavier.

Was I cool with that? Um . . . no. I am too cheap to give away all my clothes.

I had to deal with BOTH if I wanted back in my old clothes. I had to discipline my diet AND be active. *But it's not faaaaaiiiiiiirrrr. Why do I have to have a slow metabolism? It's so haaard. Why can't I keep up with the Kardashians? Whaaaaaaaaa!!!!!*

I had to make a choice. Whine about the injustice of it all and waste precious time or get to work. Be disciplined in BOTH areas.

This approach takes a lot of time. I can't eat whatever flies my direction. I can't order Gluten-Free pizza from Palio's every other night so I don't have to cook. I have to make lists and shop and cook meals ahead. I had to figure out that my crock-pot was good for something other than a place to stash extra napkins. Who knew? But, with planning and a routine, it isn't nearly as hard as it was in the beginning.

We don't have to do social media if we write fiction. We don't even have to blog. We can rely on just the quality of the book. Yet, if we pair a great book with a great platform, we vastly improve our odds of reaching or exceeding our career goals faster. Just like I could lose weight with only exercise or with only healthy eating IF I wanted to lose the weight in four years. If I wanted to lose it in 8 months? I had to do both.

Whether it is working out or writing or social media, one of the things I've noticed is that all my bad habits bubble to the surface the second I dare to strive for a life of excellence. When I decided to really do this writer thing, I had to face my fear, my insecurity, and my ugliness. I had to take a hard look at my character.

I used to be an instant gratification gal. I wanted to write a book, find an agent on the first round and be retired in the French Riviera by the end of the year.

Writing has taught me patience.

When I started my first novel, I thought I knew everything about writing.

Rejection has taught me humility.

When I began blogging, I felt very alone.

Failure taught me to focus more on community.

There are social media people who will sell you *20 Ways to Rule the World and Have a Zillion Followers.* To me, I think those folk appeal to the people who buy the *Shake Weight* and the *Chocolate Diet.* *Nudges Shake Weight under desk and out of sight.*

There is no magic pill to give us a beautiful body, and there is no social media magic that can make us best-sellers. But, to dismiss social media is like trying to get in shape without the benefit of a gym. Treadmills, barbells and StairMasters are far from gimmicks, and will get us in shape faster. But these tools require work, sacrifice and time management. Blogging will build our name, brand and reputation, but it too requires sweat equity. It will force us to look at our schedule and ask the hard questions.

Do I *really* not have enough time? Or is that just an excuse?

Today I sent my resignation to my Rotary Club. I have been a Rotarian for almost 7 years. I love Rotary, but I love writing more. It hurts to tell those friends that I won't be spending every week with them.

As baby writers, we want the freedom to choose. When we mature, we make choices that bring freedom. In the beginning of my writing career, I didn't want to tell anyone "no" and would work myself into the ground to please others. Eventually, though, I had to get to a point that I could make the tough decisions knowing that I would reap benefits later.

We have to make a choice; either the freedom to choose or the choices that bring freedom. One is short-term and the other likely won't see harvest for years to come.

It is hard to do without that $100 a week we put into savings, but trust me that it is far harder to go to work every day at age 70 and try to scrape a living out of a Social Security check. Hard work dedicated to our books and our platform is an investment. Good investments require sacrifice. It will be worth it, and I am here to support you and encourage you every step of the way.

Great Bloggers are Community-Builders—Lesson Twelve

By now, I hope you guys fully understand that there are only two things we authors can control—product and platform. Our main concern is to write a book that consumers will want to buy. No matter how great our social media platform, we can't wrap a bow around dog poo and call it a rainbow.

Blogging is our chance to beat the odds, but it's gonna require work. How much work, depends on our approach. Blogging is a totally different form of writing, and part of why many writers get overwhelmed is that they fail to appreciate what is at the heart of blogging.

What exactly is a blog anyway?

Blog was a term that evolved from two words—web and log. Web log, became blog.

Many people make the mistake of thinking that blogs are on-line journals. No. That is an on-line journal. Blogs serve the readers FIRST. But, many people also believe that blogs are on-line articles. Not necessarily.

Blogging in the form of articles is great if you are a NF author. I use my blogs to get the information wandering through my gray matter down on the page. I then harvest the blogs for my books and workshops. Providing consistent, excellent information can help build our reputation as an expert, which is essential for selling NF. No one cares about our book in the beginning. Platform built via blogging can make them care.

But, if you are a fiction author, writing three articles a week might wear you out, so I am going to let you in on a really cool secret that will help you be more creative with your blog and will also save time.

Feed the need.

First, we need to look at WHY people are on social media. Why are people gravitating by the millions to social media? Information and entertainment.

Noooooo. Why are they really on social media?

Community.

Nooooo. Why are they really, really on social media?

Purpose.

Most people, when they start a blog, stop at that first tier of wants/needs. Hey, I did. The problem with this approach is that it isn't primal. It isn't resonating at the deepest emotional level. A blog that is essentially a journal does nothing to serve the reader, so we'll just ignore that. But, our blogs can be more than just article after article.

One of the funniest things I have witnessed in fiction authors is that we have the imagination to create entirely new worlds and civilizations, but then we seem to lose all creativity when we try to start a blog. So right now we are going to pry apart the blog like a cheap piñata and go for the gooey candy guts inside. Blogging, aside from your actual novel, should be the highlight of your day. It should be FUN. If we aren't about fun, then we need to forget this writing thing and stay working in Corporate America, the place where meetings and metrics steal our will to live little by little.

Blogging needs to work with our personality.

When it comes to blogging, a lot is going to depend on your writing personality. I have members of my critique group who can bust out three thousand words, and that is just a warm up. I happen to be a talker. I talk through things. So when I write my blogs, I am not writing so much as taking dictation from the voices in my head. Boy that just made you guys feel reeeeaal secure.

The voices haven't told me to kill anyone . . . yet.

I know my subject matter so well that the words just pour onto the page. That's how I can be so prolific. Maybe you aren't this prolific. Maybe you struggle and have to research and outline and write and rewrite. Perhaps blogging is making you hate me, your dog, and every fluffy kitten you see you want to punch in the face. It happens. Guess what? Change tactics. It is permitted. Blogging police will not take you to jail.

We control our blogs. Our blogs don't control us.

News flash. You can change topics . . . and our head WON'T explode. Seriously. It will not rip the fabric of my reality if you are blogging about writing now, but since it is making you crazy you decide to blog about history or gardening. We are smart. We'll catch up. This is why your blog's title should always be your brand—YOUR NAME. Then we are following and supporting YOU, not your topic. We are loyal to YOU first.

If I have a blog called *Fairy Rainbow Glitter Dreams* I, first of all, give every one of you permission to slap me. My NAME is most important. But aside from diluting my brand by using *Fairy Rainbow Glitter Dreams*, I am also pigeon-holing my content. I'm severely limiting my topics. I am branding a *concept* not *me.*

If I blog on all things fantasy and fairy and it doesn't do well, how do I change tactics? I really can't. Also, I could get so sick of fairies I want to punch them in the face . . . with a fluffy kitten. Again, I have painted myself in a corner on content by naming my blog *Fairy Rainbow Glitter Dreams.* When we use our NAME, then our blog posts have more freedom to be dynamic and change as we change and as our audience grows.

If I change topics, do I need to start an entirely new blog?

It is a total time suck to start a new blog if we want to talk on a different subject. It is a formula to be spread so thinly that you want to scream. My goal is to have you funneling all your work into one place—YOU. If our blog is under our name and we want to change topics, just ease readers into the change. Gradually shift topics, or just blog another day on the different topic. That simple.

Our psyche will not fracture if you blog on writing on Monday and then add in history on Wednesday. If we don't care about history, we will just read Monday. We won't need therapy. Honest. Also, if you find that your history blog is far more easy and enjoyable to write and it is gaining a following, you can eventually either stop blogging on writing, or make both days history. By building everything under your name, you now have a freedom to be flexible.

But what if I named my blog something specific like *Fairy Rainbow Glitter Dreams*?

Um . . . change it. My blog started out as Warrior Writers and it is in the URL. In the beginning I didn't know as much. I learned a lot through trial and error. Just change the blog's title to your name, and make sure your name is in the tags *every post.* Most people won't pay a lot of attention to the URL name. As long as your name is in all of your tags, your blog will show up on a Google search for your name.

But Kristen, I am afraid I just don't have TIME to blog and write.

Many of you reading this book might be concerned that you just don't have time to write blogs AND a novel. I feel your pain. I have a curtain-climber who actively pursues death every waking moment. Trust me when I say that it *does* affect my writing time.

If you have a hard time getting out word count without it seriously cutting into the time you have for writing your novel, does it mean blogging isn't for you?

No. You just have to do things a bit differently. First, I want you to embed this in your brain:

No matter how much we try, our blog cannot do what only our book can. Only our book can make readers fall in love with our characters and our plot. Our brand is US, not our books.

Books and topics just make up the larger brand . . . YOU.

I am about to say something shocking. Great bloggers are not necessarily great writers. **Great bloggers are master community-builders.** I have actually been saying this for almost two years.

We can be excellent writers and our blog can be failing. Go look at my first blogs if you want a great example of a one-way dialogue. I was writing "articles." I was only getting to that first layer of wants—entertainment and information. What I didn't yet understand was that a blog isn't just about information and entertainment. It was about creating a community. How did I learn this? I read a lot of other blogs. I watched what successful bloggers were doing that I wasn't.

Blogging is to make followers fall in love with US. Part of defining our brand is figuring out what kind of community-builders we long to be. Blogging, if done correctly, becomes kind of a community watering hole for our followers, and we are the Host with the Most who throws the best parties. Great bloggers get people sharing opinions and feedback and they actively encourage a two-way dialogue. Our blog not only is popular because of content, but it is also a place we like to go on an emotional level, because the blogger is filling our deeper needs—community and purpose.

But how? Glad you asked.

Blogging—Some Nuts and Bolts—Lesson Thirteen

Yes, I am going to teach you how to write a blog. Contrary to popular belief, we are not instant writers the second we eek through high school English and make an A on that drivel we cut and pasted together with note cards, ballpoint pen and sadness. Yes, I am old enough to have used index cards for my high school....

cough

Okay, *college* papers.

Journalism is a specific kind of writing and *gasp* people even go to college to learn Journalism. The insanity! Guess what? Writing a novel is a specific craft, with skills that must be *learned* with much crying, drinking and gnashing of teeth. Would we all love to be that person who knows this stuff instinctively and rockets to the top of the best-selling list with the novel he wrote on cocktail napkins while waiting tables and selling pirated DVDs? YES! But I assume most of us wish we were born with *Gates* or *Kennedy* as a last name, too.

Hey, if wishes were fishes, we'd all cast a net.

Here's the deal. Wishing we were born instant geniuses is about as productive as wishing we were born into royalty. What does this mean? It means put on the grungy pants. It's time to do some work.

Blogging is a totally different kind of writing. I see a lot of great "writing" on sucky blogs. Blogging is different.

Think Journalism. When you want to know about the nuclear reactor in Japan, do you want to open the paper to:

The sun crept over the eastern mountains and glittered across the wreckage below. People, dying and wounded threaded the streets, their eyes unfocused and mouths limp. The tsunami had dragged hope and loved ones back into the dark churning belly of the sea. The reactor belched black death into air already thick with fear.

NO! That is creative writing, not journalism. We want the facts. We want to first know how we can help our Japanese friends fast, and

148

then, we ultimately want to know how and if and when the disaster might affect us.

When we blog, it is a very specific kind of writing that is meant to be fast, easy, and portable. Like journalism, blogging has to capture the attention of readers with the attention span of a squirrel with severe ADD that is high off Thin Mints and crack cocaine.

Many writers are not approaching their blog with the appropriate style of writing, and frankly, that is why you are exhausted and covered in strange bruises.

A couple chapters ago, I referenced Chef Gordon Ramsay. I LOVE Kitchen Nightmares. Gordon Ramsay ROCKS. What I really, really love about this show, is that there are so many lessons that cross-apply to writers.

There is one particular episode I saw two years ago that comes to mind. This owner loved to cook, and so he opened a restaurant. Pretty soon, however, he was chin-deep in debt and sinking fast. The owner/chef happened to be a huge fan of Ramsay, and when Gordon showed, the owner proudly displayed the shelves of Gordon Ramsay cookbooks that he had been using for the menu at the restaurant.

Ramsay nearly fell over. Want to know why? Those recipes were too complex for a restaurant. They were written for someone cooking at home for a family or a party. No chef would ever be able to turn out quality food in a timely fashion using recipes so intricate.

This owner-chef needed recipes that fit his needs—serving large groups of people tasty food in a timely manner. Our blogs are the same. If we approach blogging with the care and intricacy of our novel or even our NF work, we are setting ourselves up to fail.

Blogging is like fast food we get through a drive-thru window. People (readers) need to be able to keep moving and still ingest and digest. If we take a moment to think about how many people read blogs, this makes sense. With the rise of PDAs, many people are reading their blogs on their phones while on stolen breaks at the workplace. If we make people work too hard for our content, they are likely to pass or put off our blogs for later.

Neither is good.

Here are some general rules about good blogs:

Blogs preferably should be short. Oh how I suck at following this rule. You can break this rule if you break it well.

Many of you guys are probably getting heart palpitations thinking you need to churn out some 1000-2000 word tome. You don't. My blogs are generally longer because I assume many of you want to learn this social media stuff before it is obsolete. Unlike me, however, most of you will not have content that you are running after like a dog chasing a car he will never catch. Thus, your posts can be shorter . . . like 250-600 words.

Blogs need to be portable (simple). Again, think fast food. Burgers, tacos, pizza. There are no drive-thrus serving *Steak au Poivre* or roasted duck with an orange reduction. THOSE DISHES AREN'T PORTABLE.

This is why I break everything down into baby food particulates you can smear in your hair and fling at the wall should you desire. Hey, social media makes me want to fling things at the wall. Might as well be something orange that is easy to see and clean up, right? Simple is better.

If you make points, illustrate with easy, visual examples, which brings me to my next point.

Blogs need to be visual.

Humans are story people. Stories resonate with our soul. We have enjoyed stories since we were sporting the latest Saber-Tooth fashions. People dig stories. Stories stick. If we are writers, then stories should not be that hard.

My blogs are so simple a brain-damaged caveman could get them. Why? Not only is it good blogging to keep things simple, but I have to be blunt. Writers are notorious for overcomplicating things. Yes! You! I know how you think, and it really is this simple. Stop making it harder than it needs to be. Visual examples and illustrations help people grasp material and *retain* it. When they *retain* they *return.*

Blogs need to generate community.

As we discussed in the previous chapter, blogs do not have to be article after article. That is a formula to wear out fast and hate your blog, hate me, and end up drinking straight from a margarita machine.

Blogs are a way to just get people talking. Humans bond by giving opinions and advice. Don't believe me? Call your mother. Like now. We'll wait.

taps toe and hums

I bet it took her less than thirty seconds to give you unsolicited advice or an opinion. Tell her Kristen says, "Hi."

Why do our mothers freely offer unsolicited therapy and opinions? Because that is how humans (including mothers) show LOVE and CARE and COMMUNITY. They give advice and opinions whether we want it or not.

If we write blogs that encourage others to give opinions and advice, that activates the warm fluffy feeling in their collective little souls. Hey, I know it does mine. I DIG giving advice. Why do you think I write a blog four days a week when I could be doing other things like dusting or paying bills or leveling up on *Bejeweled*?

When we approach our blogs with the idea of creating a community rather than selling our book the results are nothing short of magical.

Ah, but we have to knuckle down and get to work. Part of being a great blogger is being dependable, and that requires we get into good habits.

Go Hard or Go Home—Blogging and Branding—Lesson Fourteen

This is a tough job. I recommend that if you have any shred of sanity you quit today. Give up. Give me a break. You want to do WHAT? Write? Play with your little imaginary friends all day? How are you going to pay rent? Survive? You call writing a JOB? Are you high? Were you born stupid, or did you take lessons?

Still here?

Good. Now that's out of the way. This job is hard. It is not for slacker losers who want to type on the computer when they feel inspired. Historically, novelists have had a mind-numbing failure rate. I believe that this is mainly because most of us are naturally lazy and have the attention span of a ferret addicted to meth. For that, my solution is simple.

PAY ATTENTION AND NAIL YOUR CAN TO A CHAIR YOU LAZY SLACKER.

Feel better? Always makes me smile.

Another reason for this failure rate? Until recently, writers only had control over part of their career.

I have said this over and over in this book. There are only two ways to sell books—good product and word of mouth. Period. Book trailers don't work. Shiny bookmarks don't work. Full-page newspaper spreads don't work. They don't make so much as a blip in the sales numbers, especially when it comes to fiction. Anyone who says otherwise is selling something. Probably ad space.

This is why I put together a book about blogging. Here is your chance to take the keys to your future and scream off in a cloud of burning rubber as the naysayers choke on your dust. Oh, but we need to make sure.

QUIT NOW, BEFORE IT'S TOO LATE.
YOU ARE DOOOOOOMED.
WHY DON'T YOU GET A REAL JOB?
DREAMS DON'T PAY THE BILLS.
What are you still doing here?

Alright. So clearly I cannot talk you into doing something practical with your life, so make sure you are doing this blogging thing the right way. For the love of all that is good put your NAME on your blog. I have had many blogs that I wanted to list in my weekly mash-up, but I couldn't find a NAME.

Now, I didn't always do things the right way. Don't believe me? Go to my blog and look in the URL.

slaps forehead

But, the thing is this. I realized it was a mistake and took steps to rectify the situation. I wasn't yet an "expert" when I chose the URL. I learned by making a lot of really dumb choices, and I display them proudly so you guys can see I wasn't born a rocket scientist. Yet, here's the deal. There are too many writers who want to be taken seriously, but they hide behind cutesy monikers and blog titles.

You can use your real name and yet still be safe. And if you are worried others will "find out" about your writing, um—*scratches head*—how did you expect to sell books? If you rocket to the top of the best-selling list, people will likely know who you are and what you write. *GASP!*

Do you spend *your* free time Googling people you know to see what they are doing in their free time? Then why do you think others are doing it to you? Just write.

All our efforts will mean next to nothing if people cannot clearly see our name. Our goal is to become branded, powerhouse authors whose NAME alone sells books. James Rollins, Stephen King and Sandra Brown regularly hit the New York Times best-selling list in pre-sales. Their books aren't even out yet and they hit the best-selling lists. Why? Their name on its own holds THAT much power.

I want you to finish this book then go run amok like little digital gangbangers. I want you slapping your NAME on everything you can. Whatever that name is that will be written on the cover of your books? THAT is your gang sign.

Slap that digital gang tag across your blog's title. If you have a clever log-line? Just put your name in front of it. *Kristen Lamb's Blog—Life's a Beach and Then You Write.* Hey, I can still be clever, but my NAME is front and center. Thing is, if you don't mark your turf? Other writers will. I had to CLAIM that Kristen Lamb was THE authority on social media for writers. If I didn't? Others would. If you write fiction? Claim that genre. You are THE writer of vampire romance. If you don't? Other writers will happily fill the vacuum.

Using our name has another benefit.

Be nice to potential readers. Don't make them have to go on a hunt for your name. That leaves an opportunity for them to go, "Hmm. Not that motivated. I guess I don't need it." Or worse. "I don't feel like looking up @FairyWriter's name, but ooh, I know THAT name. I'll buy her book. She doesn't make me WORK."

Got your digital spray paint? Good.

When you finish this book, go put your name in your blog title. Then, go put your name in the tags on every post you have. Go "spray paint" your digital turf and make it yours.

Bandanas and gold jewelry are your call.

In the end, either we are here to do this thing for real or we are just playing around. If we are on social media then it needs to be with the purpose of building a platform so that we have greater odds of success down the road. Help others get to know you and your content so that one day your name alone is all people need to know the book is worth full price.

Feel free to stop by my blog and whine about the injustice of it all. You guys are my peeps, and we can just get it out here. Friend me on Facebook, and I will even send you a digital daiquiri to help you drown your sorrow. Maybe even give you digital liquid courage to tell the world you are—gasp—a *WRITER.* What's next? *PORN?*

It really doesn't have to be as big of a deal as we make it. I know this is scary, but we need to just dive in. Do this thing for real. I hope I have given you plenty of tools to make the most of your time. In the post-industrial revolution, we have to me more efficient than ever.

Earlier, I introduced you to the veiled world of supernatural creatures bent on distraction and destruction. We can have all the insight in the world about how to write amazing, world-changing blogs, but we still have to sit our butt in the chair and do the work. Work? Yes, work. Not only on our blogs, either.

Being More Productive—Taking on the Procrastination Pixies by...Eating Frogs?—Lesson Fifteen

One of the challenges of being a professional author-blogger is that there are so many cool activities that look a lot like "work" but are actually a Procrastination Pixie in disguise. There is so much busy-work that can just eat up huge chunks of time, leaving us little meaningful progress to show for all our effort. As writers we must always be gauging what is really most important. Face it. We have a lot of essential tasks for our writing job alone—writing, reading, researching, marketing, promoting, socializing on FB, blogging, tweeting, editing, revising, plotting, planning, expensive therapy, etc.

These are all jobs added on top of our day job, running a home, cleaning, cooking, laundry, church, babies, spouses, fitness, and so on and so forth. All these tasks must get done, and all these areas need tending. That is true. But, not all of them have the same priority.

There can be a lot of emotional distancing when it comes to being a writer, especially when we are new. Our dream is new and shiny....yet often not taken seriously by others. Most of the time, if we aren't careful, we won't take it seriously either. If we aren't mindful, we will allow busy-work to interfere with diving in and grabbing our dream by the horns.

Every day is a challenge for me to manage time, to learn to say no, and to focus. I am not where I want to be, but I certainly am not where I was. Compared to most people, I am actually pretty productive, so we are going to talk about increasing productivity. Get the most output for the minimal time input.

Understand that there is a difference between activity and productivity.

One of the most common Procrastination Pixies falls under the genus species name, *Activia Pixius Busyworkus*. This pixie masquerades itself as a really great use of time, but, in reality, is a total time-suck that can have you scrapbooking by lunch. What does an Activia Pixius look like? The genus includes, but is not limited to, thank you notes three months after Christmas, watching old home movies, organizing baby pictures, and quality time with the Thigh Master you bought in 1994. Basically any chore that made you groan and roll your eyes until it came time to sit and write is guaranteed to be an Activius Pixius. You make a vow to write, and suddenly that junk drawer that hasn't bothered you for the past six months is calling out to you like a siren. Strap yourself to the mast (office chair) and plug your ears. Your junk drawer has more layers than the Triassic Period, and I'll bet there are a few stray Jelly Belly Jelly Beans sealed in amber below the napkins from Chik-fil-a you are too cheap to throw away but never use.

Oh, wait…maybe that's my drawer. You get the point.

I have to make a conscious effort to focus on the meaningful tasks of the day. If we aren't deliberate, the Activia Pixius will whisk us off to a hall closet to sort Goodwill donations in three seconds flat.

At the end of the day you might be able to eat off your floors, but sadly, shiny floors do not impress agents. I know, I asked the one locked in my closet—ha ha ha ha! Kidding. My closets are way too cluttered to hold an agent!

Organized cabinets do not sell books. They might make more room for all the books left unsold, but that's about it. A good way to avoid the snares of the Activia Pixius is to make goals. Real goals. FROG Goals.

Eat that Frog

One of my all-time favorite books is *Eat that Frog—21 Great Ways to Stop Procrastinating and Get More Done in Less Time* by Brian Tracy. This is a really great book, not only because of the advice, but it is short…with big print. Easy read. Actually Tracy's book changed my life. I know when I start using his methods I can take over the world in a day. Okay maybe not take it over, but at least give it a good pillow-fluffing.

Years ago, I would write my Things to Do list. I would write down everything that needed to be done, and would start with the easy things first. Right? WRONG! Brian instructs we do the opposite. Place your FROGS at the top of the page. Frogs are the tasks you dread. The bigger, the uglier, and the slimier that Frog is, the closer we need to put it to the top.

We do these FIRST. We must face our fears. Dive headlong into those tasks we dread. We are not allowed to do anything else on the list until we take out the Frogs with extreme prejudice. Two big writer frogs? Word count on the book and BLOGS. Eat them. Now. Get some ketchup if you have to.

After you eat your Frogs, then you can have "dessert." Then feel free to do the dishes, read other blogs, chat on Facebook, etc. All these other chores need to be done. Hey, my husband has grown kind of fond of eating and having clean socks. So have I. But I need to always be careful that I am not putting these tasks ahead of writing and blogging that must get done. And, actually, it is very liberating to annihilate your Frogs first. It takes away this giant anvil hanging over your head. Often the other tasks will go far quicker because now there is nothing to avoid, no Frog to make you drag your feet while folding the towels.

When we retool how we prioritize, the results are impressive.

All right. I hope you feel super prepared to take over the Internet. But, before you cut loose, there is an important topic we need to discuss. Jerks. The question isn't *if* we will have to deal with these people, as much as it is *when* we will be forced to deal with them, especially when we are blogging. Expect a ranter, a hater or an all-out TROLL to spread his nastiness all over your pretty comments section. We cannot bait, and must be professional at all times. Here's to being prepared.

Kristen Lamb

The Character of the Successful Writer—A New Level or a New Devil?—Lesson Sixteen

I have an amazing opportunity to pass on some wisdom I hope will change your life as much as it has mine. My books and blogs are dedicated to helping the human writer. Why do I say human? Because, as I mentioned in the introduction, we are more than robots sitting in front of a computer pounding out word count. We have fears and hopes and dreams and bad habits. We are all targets of Crappy Excuse Trolls and Procrastination Pixies.

It's time we talk about character. There are a lot of people in the world with the talent to take them straight to the top, but they lack the character to stay there. I hate to admit it, but I was probably one of those people. Writing and especially blogging, for me, has been a journey of developing my character as much as it has been about growing in my craft.

I've already confessed that in the not-so-distant past, I was the reigning Queen of Do It Later Land, a sad realm paved with good intentions, nestled between the Post-It Note Mountains. For years, I was better at meddling in the affairs of others than focusing on my own life. Why? I didn't have the right perspective when it came to my own problems. I dwelled on my failures and mitigated my success. I didn't have the proper relationship with failure. Instead of looking at my failures as learning experiences, I felt it was proof that I was a loser and nothing good would ever come my way.

I was so negative, I couldn't take my own company, and I had no clue how I was sabotaging my own success. The more I focused on failure, the more failure came my way. My life was filled with toxic people, and why wouldn't it be? I was gravitating to people just like me...negative, hopeless, and always living in expectation of failure. I

158

had this horrible belief that, if I never expected anything, I could never be disappointed. Those were dark years, but I thank God every day for them. Why? Because I learned to view dark times and dark people differently.

Film develops in a dark room. Character develops in dark places. So today we are going to learn some Attitude Alchemy by changing hardships from loadstones to steps in a golden staircase.

Jerks are Good for Us

I know! Hard to believe. The day I understood this principle was the day my life began to change.

All of us have areas of our character that need to improve; rough edges that, left alone, will always be rough, making it impossible for the best aspects of who we are to shine through. First, how does coal become a diamond? Pressure! Lots of pressure! Even still. Ever seen a diamond dug out of the ground? It isn't exactly ready to be set in an engagement ring. It looks like a dirty hunk of glass. It needs to be....CUT! What cuts diamonds? Other diamonds...**low grade industrial diamonds that will never be good for anything but their ability to be highly abrasive.** Jerks are the low grade industrial diamonds that shape the facets of our character. We cannot shine until we are cut, and cut again and again.

As writers, prepare to deal with a lot of jerks. When we start out, most of us are dirty, rough hunks of glass. For most of us, family will be the first line of industrial diamonds. Yes, they are likely going to roll their eyes and have sarcastic comments. They may even sabotage. We can choose to feel like a victim, or we can believe they are shaping our character. Do we love writing enough to continue? Or are we being a people pleaser who will quit the second someone has something nasty to say? My family's sarcasm made me a finisher. I had never been one of those before, and that massive flaw in my character had been a huge stumbling block barring the way to genuine success. Hah! My family thought they would stop me, but what did they really do? They polished that flaw out of my character.

Blogging will help you develop thick skin much faster. How? We have to put ourselves out there for better or worse. There will be critics. The good news, however, is that blogging offers us practice dealing with all kinds of criticism. We can silence that inner critic by meeting deadlines and building a regular following. We can silence well-

159

meaning friends and family by being able to tangibly demonstrate we are serious about our career. We can even learn to ignore negative or even hurtful people when—gasp—we have that hater who finds our blog and feels the need to tell us how much we suck. Blogging is a wonderful training ground for the career author, namely because blogging will always put you in contact with jerks (you can minimize how many by following my lessons).

I can attest that when you decide to become a writer, jerks will come out of the woodwork. Join a critique group and there is a quota that every group have at least one jack@$$. Another layer of industrial diamonds.

BZZZZZZZZZZZZTTTTTTTTT Owiiieeeee!!!!! No! Ouch! You're a writer too! I thought you'd say nice things and be supportive! Ahhhhhhhhh!!!!!

The first time I read my work for critique, I thought I was going to throw up in my shoes. But I was so proud of what I had written. Even though my family was no longer speaking to me, I finished a novel. It was the first thing I had ever stuck to. I brought it to critique so I could send it to an agent.

There was a published writer who took my pages and threw them in the air and said, "This is crap." The scent of blood filled the water and the sharks circled.

I got slaughtered.

I gritted my teeth, determined they would not break me. Somehow I made it through the rest of the session then stumbled through the parking lot to my car and cried. I so wanted to run away and give up, but that was what I had always done in the past. I dried my tears and resolved to prove I could write and write well. I refined and read and studied until the pieces I brought were polished perfect. My prose became the strongest in the group.

BZZZZZZZZZZZTTTTTTTTTT Aggghhhhhhhhh!!!!

Once you make it past the critique group, you will have to likely endure the agents. Most will send you a form letter and, if you are lucky, they will even spell your name correctly. It hurts. But again, this process is cutting facets so you can shine brighter. Maybe you need to read more or take more writing classes. Maybe, because of fear, you aren't writing in a genre you really love, so your voice isn't developing. Perhaps your platform isn't as strong as it needs to be and needs more time and work.

We can take all those "No's" as proof we are a failure, or we can take that and use it to change... *BZZZZZZZZZTTTTTTTTTTTTTTT OWWW NOT THAT!!!!! AGHHHHH!!!!*

I would love to promise that your career will be all rainbows and sunshine, but that would be doing you a great disservice. Even when you get published, and probably especially when you get published, there will still be jerks. Hopefully, I can help you minimize this, but we can't guarantee everyone will love us. My advice is to expect the best, but plan for the worst. Plan for when jerks write hateful stuff on your FB page and your blog. Brace for that person with nothing better to do than, to write you nasty e-mails or post blistering reviews about your books. Plan for it then accept that it's not personal. It's part of the job and, at the end of the day? It happens to even the best of us. It's happened to me.

Candace Havens (who is an amazing author and one of THE most awesome people in the world) showed up to a book signing in tears after someone posted a horrible, eviscerating review on Amazon. Another story. I have never seen a writer give more effort to teaching new writers than NY Times Best-Selling Author Bob Mayer. Bob had a workshop participant act so badly I seriously expected Bob to start speaking in tongues. He handled it with class, but I know he was deeply hurt by a writer he was trying very hard to help.

Jerks are part of life, and they can be a new devil or can bring a new level. The choice is ours.

Jerks can test our commitment level. They can challenge our convictions or even make us angry because they speak a truth we are scared to face. Whenever something makes me angry, I stop and ask why it bothered me. Jerks can teach us how to set effective boundaries. In Kindergarten we get taught to be nice to everyone. It's a good principle to follow, and most people are respectful. But, being nice doesn't mean we give carte blanche to people who want to tear through and wreck our lives and be hateful and disrespectful.

First, I will say that not everyone will like us, which totally stinks. I know. If someone disagrees or writes a bad review, you must ignore it then promptly call your closest friends for cupcakes and happy hour. If you feel you must say something, you must wait until you are calm. Then, there is only ONE acceptable response to a negative comment or a bad review. You must *thank* them for taking the time to give an opinion. That's it. Nothing more. No defending. Back away from the keyboard. More than one author career has been wrecked by an on-line meltdown. It isn't worth it.

Ah, but what about the trolls? Those folk who only want to spread hurt and hate. How do we handle them?

Sometimes we have to set boundaries, and that isn't always pleasant. Recently, I had to unfollow someone on FB. I NEVER have to do that. But, he was bullying me and my friends and kicking sand in their faces. He wrote hateful comments on my blog and even wrote a blog calling me all sorts of ridiculous unfair names. But, he was teaching me a lesson that I have struggled with all my life. When do we stop being polite and put our foot down? Was I going to cave in what I believe, or was I going to water down my humor so he would not be offended? I happen to believe that a sense of humor is the sign of a healthy society (and person). This individual was challenging that belief. Would I compromise?

No. I wouldn't. And I wasn't going to permit him to bully me or any of my followers.

If we want to be NY Times best-selling authors (and many of us do), it stands to reason that we will have to be effective at setting and enforcing boundaries. We will need to be disciplined and committed and believe in our work and ourselves. All those jerks along the way just *BZZZZZZZTTTTTTTTTTTT*ed off all the rough edges.

So the next time someone kicks sand in your face, you can get upset, or just smile and think...*BBZZZZZZTTTTTTT Boy are you gonna make me shine!* It isn't easy and it isn't instinctive, but the activities that are contrary to our nature and what we want to do generally are the best for us.

Lifting weights, eating broccoli or even giving up a movie with friends to make word count are not always the things that we want to do, but they take us a step closer to the big goal. Same with how we handle jerks. We can give in and cry and whine and go tell all our friends how we are picked on, or we can think, *A new level or a new devil? I choose another level. Bring it on. The more you grind, the brighter I'll SHINE! Give it your best!*

We are all pretty aware of jerks, but in this next lesson we are going to explore some ways to improve what I call our "Likability

Quotient." Being likable is probably the best way to build a successful social media platform.

Ten Ways to Raise Your Likeability Quotient—Lesson Seventeen

My social media methods rely heavily on learning to be part of a team, and, as we have discussed before, this is very contrary to traditional marketing. I believe social media works like a barn-raising. Everyone does a little bit for the good of the whole. Even just being mindful to do small things makes a huge difference in the long-run.

One of the biggest obstacles we face in social media is that we do have to limit the self-promotion. It turns people off, and they really aren't likely to listen when we go around tooting our own horn. What do we do then? We do what is counterintuitive. We support others.

The single largest determining factor as to whether a person will succeed or not on social media is our L.Q. Heard of I.Q.? Well, L.Q. is your Likeability Quotient.

We don't care how smart you are as much as we care if we LIKE you. When working on our social media platform, the ever-present questions should always be:

Do people like me?

I know it sounds crazy, but it is true. And there is no need to panic. Calm down. You don't need to hide all your D&D books and tell your geeky friends to get in the closet. This isn't high school, where popularity is based on stupid stuff.

Likability is important. Why? We hang out with people we like. We promote them. We go out of our way for them. We want them to succeed.

Our information can be the best on the web, but when pitted against another blogger with not-as-great-information, but she connects to readers and we don't? The likable blogger will win. If she promotes others, and we don't? Again, she will win.

Being an excellent writer is not enough. When we get out on

164

social media (or even launch a blog) we must make sure we have good content. That is a no-brainer. I don't know about you guys, but find it hard to like people in person who ramble or talk to hear the sound of their own voice. On the web, I like substance just as much.

But, in addition to that great content, we must actively work on how others perceive us. We must become likable. How to we become likable? We serve others first. Remember the barn-raising? Help them raise their barn, and most people will be more than happy to return the favor.

My Top 10 Ways to Raise Your L.Q.:

1. If we are on Twitter and we know an author writes great blogs, RT (retweet) for them. It only takes a minute of time, and it earns you a reputation of being an edifier and a team player.

2. Comment on blogs. A healthy comments section is a sign of a healthy blog. Comments are encouraging to bloggers who take a lot of time to craft meaningful posts. When readers take time to comment, it has the potential to generate dialogue. Dialogue is critical for a blog to thrive. I want comments on my blog, so I go out of my way to comment on the blogs of others.

3. Reply to comments on our own blogs. I wish I could reply to every single last person who takes the time to leave a comment. My followers have no idea how much they make my day when they take the time to post feedback, compliments or even their opinions on my blog. Remember in social media, our goal is to form relationships. Relationships are two-way streets. In the beginning, I responded to every comment. Now? I still try to respond to as many as I can. People need to know we are there and that we are vested.

4. Visit the sites of those who post in your comments. You guys might not be aware, but I am always on the lookout for great blogs for the mash-up. I look to people who comment on my blog, FIRST. I regularly click on the websites and blogs of those in my comments section, especially if you link to one of my posts.

5. Embed trackbacks (hyperlinks)...um the blue thingies. Link to other blogs you like. Link to books you like. Hey, we need all the help we can get these days. There are A LOT of choices. Mash-ups (lists of favorite links/blogs) and even recommendations are a great way to help out other writers and generate more traffic to your blog at the same time. Everyone wins.

165

6. Blog about your favorite books, then link to that author's book, home page or blog. Need blogging ideas? Go out of your way to promote others. Part of why I talk so much about Bob Mayer, James Scott Bell, Les Edgerton, Donald Maass, Jessica Morrell, Blake Snyder, Christopher Vogler, and Larry Brooks is because these writers are my heroes. I believe that these are the best teachers in the industry. Now, instead of them having to go out and self-promote I have gifted them with the best gift a writer can have—a genuine word-of-mouth recommendation from a fan. Make life easy on other authors, and who knows? They might one day love to return the favor.

7. When you see a blog/book you like, take a moment to tweet the post or repost the link on your FB page. This helps the blogger/author gain exposure she otherwise wouldn't have. It also benefits people in your circle of friends in that you are acting as a filter for great information, which also helps your platform grow because people trust you for quality goods.

8. Openly praise. When I see a writer post a blog, I go out of my way to open, scan and take a look. Then, when I post, I make sure to add a, "Great post!" or a, "Very interesting!" Trust me. People remember an authentic compliment.

9. Repost someone else's blog. Some people might get weird about this, but this is an amazing way to spread influence for you and the blogger you repost. Have the flu? Power outage and you don't know how you will get a blog together in time? No worries. Just repost. How do you do this?

Give the title of the blog, and *make it very clear you are reposting someone else's content.* Only give the first couple paragraphs, enough to hook a reader. Then add a hyperlink to the original blog. Now you have a blog post, and the blogger you promoted now has exposure to your regular followers. I gain a lot of subscriptions this way. There are some people who had never heard of me until Marilag Lubag (Hi Marilag!) reposted one of my blogs. Her readers followed the hyperlink, loved my blog (in its entirety), and I have new fans. Yippppeeee!

10. At least hit the "Like" button. I know that sometimes I read blogs on my phone and I really don't feel like trying to type out a compliment. I have a touch screen and there is an auto-correct function. My compliment would probably look like this:

I loved your blood. You make so many grape poinsettias and I wish I wood have fought of it. Grape stuff. Looking forehead to next leek's blood.

So if you don't want a blogger thinking you want to "leak their blood" instead of "read their blog" it is fine. Hit the "Like" button. Takes two seconds and it encourages the writer who put their effort into the blonde . . . blood . . . blog. And they WILL remember your face.

You know, I didn't always do things the right way. In the beginning, my blogs sounded more like lectures. Was I stuck up? No. Was I insecure and waiting for the digital cabbages to come flying through the screen? Yes. Fear of saying the wrong thing or sounding stupid or making a mistake can keep us from genuinely interacting. But when we fail to interact, what others see is a snob, not someone who is literally terrified that both feet will fly in her mouth. I know it doesn't make sense, but humans are self-centered, insecure and neurotic.

If someone makes a weird face, we automatically assume they are looking at our fat thighs (Okay, maybe that is just me). We don't stop to think that person might be shy. Why? Because we are paranoid narcissists and like to believe we influence everything. It's a control thing. You know I am right. You, in the back. Didn't I see you lurking on my blog? We do like you. You just were so quiet you blended in with HTML. Come hang out. Have a snack.

Being likable is far easier than it seems. I guarantee you that if you just employ a handful of those ten tactics your following will improve tremendously. Why? Because you will be giving others what we all desperately need—support, validation, compliments. In the end, our blog cannot make people love our books, but it *can* make them adore us. Being likable is essential to building that loyal following who will gladly be your biggest cheerleaders.

Kristen Lamb

Are You Committed to Your Writing? Or Just "Shacking Up?"—Lesson Eighteen

We just talked about how jerks can test our commitment level, so it is a good time to discuss exactly how devoted we are to our dream of being successful authors.

In this, our final blogging lesson, it's time to tie blogging and writing together. It is time to ask the tough question. Are you "shacking up" with your dream of writing for a living? Or are you really ready to make a commitment…like for real? *ARE YOU THERE BLOG? IT'S ME, WRITER.* I'm ready to take the plunge!

In my years of working with writers, I have run across literally hundreds of individuals who claim to want to be best-selling career authors. But, over time, it soon became clear that they were more in love with the "idea" of writing than the actual work, commitment and life that went with it, which includes building their author brand and blogging.

In effect, they were shacking up with their novel, enjoying the "dream with benefits." Wink, wink, nod, nod. Don't believe me? Hmmmmm. I have no idea why my crazy brain thought of this scenario, but it might feel painfully familiar.

Welcome to the first episode of *As the Page Turns…*
Cue dramatic music

Novel: Why haven't you called? Last January you said you were going to spend time with me every day.

Writer: I know Baby, and I'm sorry. I've been a real jerk.

Novel: I have called out to you, and you never answer. I feel like you are shutting me out. Where have you been? You aren't even blogging. You know, blogging can bring us closer together. Really, it can.

Writer: You know. Busy. Work has really been a killer, and then

168

I had some projects around the house and I've been meaning to spend time—to write—to blog—

Novel: You just don't care. You don't care about our love anymore. I used to be your whole world. You were so excited about me and wanted to blog and Facebook and Twitter all about me, but now you won't even admit you're a writer.

Writer: No, no, Baby, don't be like that. I'm trying to do better. I just can't get my family to support our relationship, and my friends, well, they just don't get my feelings for you. I'm not hiding...it's just complicated. That's all.

Novel: It isn't complicated at all. Do you love me?

Writer: Of course. With all my heart and soul I love you. I knew I was born for you from the time I was small. I am happiest when I am with you.

Novel: Then help me understand, because I just don't get it. You say you love me that you want our future to be together. You say you want to be with me all day every day, and yet you never write and you leave me alone most of the year. You won't tell your friends and family we are in a relationship, you hid me from your social feeds and you only visit me when it is convenient.

Writer: No it isn't like that...

Novel: It IS like that. When are you going to commit for real?

Writer: January 1st. I am going to give you so much attention you will get sick of me. I promise. I will even get an agent for us.

Novel: I've heard that before, and I'm not falling for it. Have you started blogging? A social media platform to let others know about me? About US? I don't need a giant 4 carat blog, just a symbol that we are together, or even a mention about me in your Twitter bio.

Writer: Um, I was going to get to that...when I got an agent.

Novel: That isn't a commitment. We have to build a community for our future. Why are you so embarrassed to tell others about me?

Writer: I just, don't want to be making a mistake. My father wanted to be a writer, too and...well it didn't work out. He was devastated. I want to just see how it goes...in private and once we get to a certain point, then I'll shout to the world that you and I are together, Baby I promise.

Novel: But you never spend time with me! And you won't tell anyone I exist! And you won't tell your twitter peeps you are committed to me, so they think you are available!

Writer: Baby, that isn't true. You know I only have eyes for you.

Novel: Oh, really. What about that yoga class? Hmmm? Or the Scentsy Candle parties you agreed to host? You could have been spending time with me, but no. They thought you were available because you were playing SINGLE. Was yoga prettier than me?

Writer: Okay, now you are just being childish. Yoga and Scentsy meant nothing to me. It was a wild fling and I am just confused right now.

Novel: Well, you better get unconfused. I want a commitment, a blog to tell everyone you are serious or we will never work. I need an hour of your time a day and I need to know we have a future. I need this, or me and the muse are gone. This year I am sticking to my guns. I want an hour a day and I want a blog and Facebook and Twitter. I want a real demonstration that you care. That...or we are finished.

Tune in for the next episode of *As the Page Turns*. Will Writer finally give Novel the commitment she deserves? How long will Novel be content to stay in the shadows? Will Novel tell Writer she is carrying his unborn climactic scene?

Okay, I'll stop. You guys get the point and I had way too much fun with that. For many of us, there is this mental block to stepping up and claiming to be a professional writer (Been there!). Being a professional writer doesn't mean that you get paid...yet. It is a mental shift. It is a shift in the relationship you have with your writing, from casual love affair to a lifelong commitment. I cannot emphasize enough how even blogging once a week can totally transform your commitment level to your dream.

So are you "shacking up" with your writing or are you committed? Just as committed relationships with people have certain behaviors, commitment to being a writer does, too. We can't work on our writing only when it is emotionally gratifying for us. We have to elevate the work and slog away day after day even when it feels like we are walking barefoot across hot coals while eating glass. Commitment means we make meaningful plans for the future. We invest time and resources. Building a social media platform lets others know we are married to this future.

I'm sorry. I would love to go to the movies, but I really have to get my word count and Monday's blog written first. Can we do a later showing?

So as we hurdle through yet another year and toward another New Year's Resolution, we need to ask ourselves if we are genuinely committed to our writing, or are we just enjoying a "dream with benefits?" The answer might sting. How do you think I knew the above dialogue so well? I wasn't always committed either. I was the world's worst "Writing Gigolo," drifting from genre to prettier new shiny genre. I would "commit" to one novel only to flirt with a new idea, and then drop the old novel like a hot potato. I wrote when I felt like it and when it was "good for me." I was a bad, bad writer. A Prose Playboy of the worst sort, but blogging helped me mend my ways. Even though I struggle with a wandering eye—Oooh! Scrapbooking!—I make sure I stay true to my one and only love. Blogging keeps me beholden to Novel. It takes work and sacrifice, but it is the greatest feeling in the world.

Kristen Lamb

Section Three—Testimonials: Does This Stuff Work?

After all of this, some of you might be wondering if all this stuff I'm teaching works? I have offered my own success stories, but I'd like to give you guys a chance to hear from other writers who have used my tactics and experienced tremendous success. I want you to know that all my methods were rigorously tested on other writers before being offered to the general public.

For instance, I would place interesting blog content at the end of a maze, and, if the writer could find it, she was allowed a second cup of coffee. I generally avoided experiments involving electroshock namely because writers are masochists, and most of them liked it. Thus, I tried to focus on positive rewards like shiny bookmarks or chocolate. I also tested various platforms. Which ones made the writers spontaneously break out in hives or lose all their hair? Did the writer curl into the fetal position when made to tweet? When placed in a puzzle, could the writer pick one pen name? Of course, there was always some caffeinated beverage placed at the end as a reward for staying on task.

My guinea pig writers sacrificed so that future writers could benefit (*No writers were permanently harmed. Okay, maybe one or two, but they were odd to start with*).

I have three testimonials to share with you, but we will begin with Piper Bayard. She was one of my first guinea pigs, and it has been an amazing experience to watch her grow as a writer and blogger, and, if anyone deserves to share her tale, it is this gal. She has used all the methods I teach to build and grow her now very popular (and FUNNY!) blog. She is a growing force on Facebook and Twitter and you are missing out if you don't go friend her as soon as possible. Here is her story.

The Guinea Pig Diaries—Piper's Story

When I stepped off the plane in Dallas for the DFW Writers Conference last April, I had no idea that I would arrive an aspiring writer and leave...a guinea pig?

I met Kristen where you always meet the people experienced in life and writing—out on the dark porch where the "bad girls" go to smoke and drink. As a recovering attorney, I knew that was where I would find the real action at the conference. Sure enough, there she was, slinging her Texas drawl with New York speed while gesticulating wildly with both hands and expounding to a group on why "a girl who finds out she's a fairy, and, oh yeah, she has daddy issues," sucked as a logline.

To be honest, I've spent most of my life being a character and living stories rather than learning to write them, so I had no idea what a logline was. This woman was either dazzling with brilliance or baffling with BS. But, either way, she was good at it, and, most importantly, she wasn't picking on me, so I stuck around. By the time she finished emitting her Death Star blast on the unsuspecting fairy writer, I knew what a logline was. Sadly, I also knew that mine sucked, too. But more importantly, everyone listening knew why our loglines sucked, and how we could fix them. Kristen was blunt and unvarnished in her delivery, but her assessments rang true. She was all about making us better writers.

Forget ego. I needed to learn what she was teaching.

The next day, I stuck to Kristen like a burr in her fetlock, taking her classes and listening as others asked her questions. She said scary words like "blog" and "hashtag," and insisted that Facebook and Twitter would change my life as surely as the microwave had changed the TV dinner. (Yes, I'm that old.)

Now, just to give you the full picture, when it came to computers, I could usually get the O-N/O-F-F switch to the O-N position and send an email, but only if that email didn't have an attachment. In my mind, *Blog* was cousin to the *Creature from the Black Lagoon*. *Hashtag* was the corned beef on my shirt after breakfast, and Facebook was a place with people who were looking for me, and not to give me a cyber-hug. And this woman was saying I had do all of them?

I tried to inhale deeply, but my best efforts were rapid and shallow. I wondered if the tote DFWWC gave me would be as effective to breathe into as a paper bag. Then the worst happened. Kristen glanced over the heads of the people I was hiding behind and asked, "Do you blog?"

Suddenly, as I stood there quivering under her laser gaze, my legs shrunk and hair sprouted all over my body. I snatched some garnish from a passing caterer's tray and fought an overwhelming compulsion to seek out a Nutri-log to hide in. What was happening to me? I tried to ask, "Umm. . . . What's a blog?" but all that came out was, "*Bweep, bweep, bweep!*" That's when we both knew. I was no "aspiring writer." I was her guinea pig.

She said, "Type up your bio and send it to me."

What was that she was holding out? A honey treat?

"Uhh. . . . Ok." Bio. Familiar word. And I didn't even have to research it to write it. Oh, sure, I was daunted at being in the fairy writer's hot seat, but what the ▓▓? You ante up or you get out of the game. So I took my best shot and wrote a nice, safe, no-one's-going-to-argue-with-this biography.

Kristen's response? "Booor - iiiing. You are a fiction writer, for God's sake! I can't understand why people who write 100,000 words of pure lies feel like they have to tell the truth in their biography. Use your imagination and try again."

So I did. I sent her 350 words of pure, unadulterated BS that was swimming around in my head at 4:00 a.m. in the middle of a SCUBA trip, and she told me, "That's more like it." Yea! A win!

"Now you need to start a blog."

"*Bweep, bweep, bweep!*" There was that four-letter word again. I chewed open a pillow and pawed madly through the fluff. That's when I knew I had a choice to make. To be, or not to be?

In twenty years of teaching belly dancing, I always told my students, "You're a dancer when you decide you're a dancer. No one gives you permission but you." It's the same with writing. There is no such thing as "aspiring." There is only doing.

So I got a copy of Kristen's book, and I took the plunge, a large pile of Timothy hay beside me to graze through while I worked. And you know what I found out? If you can talk, you can blog. Blogging is just talking to people. It's probably the easiest writing you could ever do. Find something you like to talk about—not yourself—and talk about it. With the Internet for research, you can even talk about it knowledgeably.

You know what's happened since this guinea pig started blogging? I now say, "I'm an author," with confidence. I now take my own writing seriously, and so do my family and friends. And when I'm chatting with folks while I'm out and about in my day, I say, "You know, I was just writing about that. . . ." Which is a great excuse to give them my business card. In no time, I found my blog voice, and now, I'm even on Facebook and Twitter. Yes, me. The O-N/O-F-F switch girl. If I can do it, you can, too.

The ubiquitous body hair receded, and I replaced the half-chewed door on my closet. (Don't hassle me. I couldn't find a Nutri-log my size, ok?) I even started feeling pretty comfortable with this social media thing. Then Kristen did it again. . . . "Would you like to write your success story?"

"*Bweep, bweep, bweep!*" I just need to gnaw this chair leg for a while. My profound thanks to Kristen Lamb for adopting me from the Writer Shelter. All my best to you folks newly finding your way. Trust me when I say Kristen's approach creates more time for writing, allowing less time for nibbling furniture. . . . Ooooh! Is she holding a strawberry?

The Cult of WANA—Peter's Story

Hello. My name is Peter St-Clair, and this is my testimony. No one ever sets out to join a cult. They join a group that shares the same world vision.

I first got involved with the WANAites by accident mid-2010 when I ran across the writings of the charismatic Prophet Lamb in the Freshly Pressed section of the Word (Press). For hours I poured over her archived teachings and began to see the error of my unholy ways. You see, I had been trying in vain for many years to establish my own teachings, and it simply wasn't working. Thankfully, the Prophet was there to set me straight. She made me realize that you have to be a good follower (on Twitter) before you can lead a successful flock of your own.

After that first day, I was hooked. As soon as I stepped into the Church of WANA, I knew that I was home.

I started showing up for the WANA Wednesday services every week, but very often I would be drawn to services the Prophet held on other days of the week, too. It always seemed that she was talking directly to me and that she somehow had the ability to discern my unvoiced fears about my own path to Writerdom. She's the type of person that has the uncanny power to look at your Face (book page) and tell you exactly what you're doing wrong in a personalized catharsis session.

Ok, I have to stop that now. I'm evidently known as the 'cult guy' in the WANA circle because of my often strange and obsessive fascination with cults (which I now blog about, thanks to Kristen), so the above sort of fits with that.

I guess the whole point of this essay is to let you know that the tips and techniques laid out in Kristen's blogs and book actually do work and quite well.

Before I joined the "Cult of WANA," I was a lost soul in a sea of new writers with no direction. I'd been planning on writing a novel for many years, but I had no idea where to start, so I never did. When I finally stumbled on to Kristen's blog, I realized I was not the only one with that problem. Her posts gave me the courage to stand up and proudly proclaim that I was a writer for the entire world to hear, or well, read. She also made a point to let me know that I didn't have to travel the road alone. The most important thing she taught me, however, was the work that should get done before I even had a finished manuscript-building my platform with social media. An *author brand*, if you will, which is a term she uses a lot.

Like most people my age, I'd had a blog for many years but wasn't getting the traffic I wanted, nor did many people comment on the posts that I had written. I never was one to write about my personal life, so I had decided early on that I would blog about my interests, which tend to bounce around quite frequently. The problem with that way of blogging is that it's hard to stay on topic, which is something a solid following pretty much requires; couple that with inconsistent posting days and long absences, what you're left with is an awesome recipe for FAIL. Which my blog was. It didn't matter how good the content may or may not have been (I won't say which ;p).

After I proclaimed my status as a writer, I started a new blog. Literally minutes after my first post, Kristen Lamb had already commented on it providing me with some much needed encouragement. How'd she know? Like I told you above, she's just *that good* at social media.

At first, I was posting two days a week, one on cults and one on the craft side of writing as I was/am learning it. Within a week or two, I was already getting more comments on posts and traffic than I ever had in the past. Some of it had to do with the fact that I was blogging consistently and on topic, but another part of it had to do with the fact that I let people on Facebook and twitter know. These are people I've come to know through re-tweets and links posted on Facebook and other blogs. It also helped that Kristen regularly featured me and other writers like Piper Bayard in her **Mash-up of Awesomeness** almost every week, which she still does.

Now I post three times a week and don't have to rely on Kristen to mention me to get comments and traffic. That's not a hit to Kristen, but rather actually a testimony to the fact that her system does work. I wish you all the best, and see you at WANA Wednesday service.

Kristen Lamb

The Six Degrees of Kristen Lamb—Susan's Story

Hi, my name is Susan Bischoff, and I'm here to tell you it's true. It's a small world—and getting smaller all the time. Are you tired of hearing that yet? Too bad. Because it's not going anywhere. Our ability to communicate just keeps growing, from language, to paper, to printing; from the Pony Express, to Federal Express; from LISTSERV to today's social media frenzy that you don't need me to tell you about—you need Kristen Lamb.

Or at least I did. When I was preparing for my debut as an author, numbers seemed so much bigger to me. I remember talking to an author friend, being awed by both her current success and her vision of the future, and I just had to frankly ask, "Aren't you going to run out of people to sell to?" Because I just couldn't see how she could have sold what she'd already sold, and yet she still expected this book to continue to sell.

Now, if it were possible to generate an exasperated, head-shaking font in a chat window, I think I'd be seeing it a lot, and certainly on this occasion when she replied, "Well, Susan, how many readers do YOU think there are?"

"I don't know, like 50,000?"

Now, kids, I don't care if you laugh at me, but that's only because I can't actually hear you.

She continued, "Then how do you explain the sales of books like Twilight and Harry Potter?"

"I don't know. I guess I just figure there are a couple million people who potentially COULD read a book, but those are the people who only read the books that everyone and/or Oprah says you HAVE to read. But when I think of like the general reading public who actually read books, I'm thinking it's like 50k?"

Suffice it to say that my friend proceeded to give me a nice

181

talking to about my world view, and, for some people, such an opening of the eyes would have left them excited about a greater range of possibility and possible success, and about the coming challenge of reaching out to all those readers out there.

It just made me queasy.

Like many, I loved writing, creating, and the idea of being an author, and felt sort of hopeless and scared about promoting, selling, and the idea of marketing. It was already bad enough when I was thinking about 50,000 readers, but now I was supposed to think about some innumerable throng of potential readers? Plus, PLUS, I was supposed to think beyond the next ten minutes and start thinking about the career I was building and how it wasn't just the readers who were shopping today, but that there would always be new readers coming up in age and crossing over from other genres?

Ouch.

In my head I could turn these imaginary people from potential readers to potential rejecters. A legion of potential rejection. A massive zombie hoard coming at me, saying no, No, NO! Reaching out to me with their boney, dream-crushing hands, their jaws hanging open to suck my will to ever write again, and me, facing off against them, with nothing but a 200 page trade paperback to defend myself, swinging wildly, but more of them keep coming up and crossing over and—

I can be a very negative person, and sometimes my imagination gets away from me just a little bit.

But note the imagery here. Why am I facing off against my potential readers? Why did I build up such negativity in my head around the word "marketing?" Why was the idea of telling people about my book such a big deal? And why was it always me, alone?

So when another writer friend said, "You should check out this book [LINK]," and the title was *We Are Not Alone—The Writer's Guide to Social Media*, you can clearly see the appeal.

Kristen's book helped me understand that I was never supposed to be able to personally reach all those potential readers out there— except maybe, someday, through my books. Social media was going to help me reach the people I could reach, touch them, inform them, entertain them, and take care of them to the point where they would want to tell people about me, and my work. And, as I read her book, I started to grasp the Flex Shampoo simplicity of it, realizing that they would tell their friends, and they would tell their friends, and so on, and so on, and so on....

Kristen not only told me where to put my social media efforts, but helped me think through the kinds of things I would want to say there. She helped me with such scary things as focusing my brand, and figuring out how to describe what I was doing—with keywords rather than nebulous ideas. To know what I wanted to say about my work and about myself as an author.

And I think it works for me. Even though I still have work to do on my Susie Social-Marketer side, months later, I can say that things are rolling along with that Flex Shampoo simplicity. Now I'm the one telling the nervous new authors, "Don't worry, the marketing stuff is not as bad as you think it is. Have you read Kristen Lamb's book yet?"

That's how I know the theory works: because I find myself workin' it for Kristen all the time. Then I hop over to the blog of a friend to whom I've recommended Kristen's book, and I see HIM recommending Kristen's book. And so on, and so on....

It seems like every time someone comes up new to me on social media and follows me, or says, "Hey, I loved your book," or tweets to tell others about a blog post I've just published, it's someone who's already connected to a handful of people I already know. So no surprise, really, that I'm talking to Piper Bayard on Twitter and Kristen shows up and tweets:

@susan_bischoff @PiperBayard It's so cool to see my peeps become tweeps :D

This shouldn't be a big surprise, Kristen, you're the one who DRAGGED us all here, kicking and screaming like toddlers in a tantrum. Piper replies:

RT @KristenLambTX: @susan_bischoff It's so cool to see my peeps become tweeps :D< I feel like such a big girl. No more social media Pullups.

Kristen has already helped so many authors navigate social media, and continues to be there with new information, inspiration and support. I can't go more than a few authors now and not find someone who's already been helped by *We Are Not Alone*, by one of her workshops, or by her blog. It's harder than trying to find a movie without Kevin Bacon in it.

Soon we'll be able to play the six degrees of @KristenLambTX game. @PiperBayard

There are so many more writers out there who have been helped by these methods, and I would love to share every one of them. I hope you come away from all of this feeling encouraged and inspired.

In Conclusion

I hope you enjoyed this selection of my social media lessons from this past year. If you don't yet own a copy of my book *We Are Not Alone—The Writer's Guide to Social Media*, I recommend you buy one, especially if you are intimidated by technology. It's an excellent resource to walk you through, step-by-step, setting up your social media platform and linking everything together so that all your energies will be focused to feeding and building your brand. Aside from a computer and an Internet connection, everything I teach is free and will only cost you time and effort. I include tips on how to write your bios, collect your content, and prepare you for success before you even open a Facebook or Twitter account. Sign up for all the major platforms with ease (my book has pictures!), and maybe even breathe new life into Facebook pages or Twitter accounts left to gather dust and spam. Invest a few dollars in your future. My methods will teach you how to connect to your readers and still have time left over to eat, sleep and write more brilliant books. At the end of the day, the entire point of all this blogging and tweeting and Facebooking is that we love to write, and we want to do everything in our power to make a career of it.

I trust this book has persuaded you to visit my blog for even more lessons on how to make social media the best experience possible. Find me on Twitter at @KristenLambTX, and I encourage you to poach my tweeps (translation: make friends with my friends). The easiest way to do this is to come join my Twibe by following the #MyWANA on Twitter. #MyWANA is a group of wonderful individuals committed to the WANA principles; the best tweeps in the Twitterverse. On #MyWANA, you can instantly connect with a group of friends who can teach, guide, and support you as you build your author platform. We are not alone!

I am also easy to find on Facebook. Send me a message. Tell me about your blogs so I can support you. If you only take one thing away from this book, I hope it is a spirit of genuine service. Here's to your future. You're gonna need shades.

Happy writing!

Until next time...

About the Author

Kristen takes her years of experience in sales & promotion and merges it with almost a decade as a writer to create a program designed to help authors construct a platform in the new paradigm of publishing. Kristen has guided writers of all levels, from unpublished green peas to NY Times best-selling big fish, how to use social media to create a solid platform and brand. Most importantly, Kristen helps authors of all levels connect to their READERS and then maintain a relationship that grows into a long-term fan base.

Currently Kristen is teaching *Blogging to Build Your Author Brand, We Are Not Alone–Social Media for the 21st Century Author* at various writer conferences across the country. Stay tuned for a workshop in your area.

187

CPSIA information can be obtained at www.ICGtesting.com

261969BV00001B/5/P